D1415429

"Me Like Goat Meat. Goat Meat Good, Mon"

In the Company of Curiosities, Anachronisms, Misfits, Innocents, and Angels

Photographs & text by
Ethan Hubbard

Book and cover design by RavenMark, Inc.
Book edited by Woodie Hartman
Printed in Korea by P. Chan & Edward, Inc.

ISBN 978-0-615-55902-5

© 2011 by Ethan Hubbard

All rights reserved. No part of this book may be reproduced,
stored, or transmitted, in any form or by any means, electronic,
mechanical, photocopying, or otherwise, without written
permission of the author.

Ethan Hubbard
P.O. Box 292, Chelsea, Vermont 05038
(802) 685-2025
ethanh@sover.net

A Craftsbury Common publication.

I lovingly dedicate this book to the memory of two dear men
who served as my adoptive fathers from 1960-2011.

Harry Smith of Waitsfield, Vermont
and
Francis Foster of Walden, Vermont

"Long may you run!"

Preface

When I was a boy of twelve, I rode my bicycle from Washington, Connecticut, to Pownal, Vermont, in a single day — a distance of 92 miles. I camped in a gravel pit as soon as I crossed the state line. I was utterly exhausted and wanted nothing but a quick fire, a hasty meal, and sleep. It was a preposterous distance for anyone, let alone a kid, to attempt in one day, especially on a bulky, one-speed Schwinn, loaded down with fifty pounds of food, clothing, sleeping bag, and tent. Weighing in at barely 95 pounds, I attacked the journey with an inner strength I didn't know I possessed — a small boy pedaling into the wind, bucking the traffic, eyes alert, heart pounding. The following morning I pedaled the 92 miles back home. My father met me at the door, and, instead of praising me for my accomplishment, browbeat me for being gone so long. He didn't even believe I had been to Vermont and called me a liar. (I am still working to offload this wound!)

Sixty years later, I still drive those 92 miles in my car to visit my family, amazed as ever that I cycled that distance as a child. Many landmarks remain: a stone table beside a cemetery where I rested, a spring where I slaked my thirst, a covered bridge in Cornwall where I celebrated my return with an impromptu jig. These are reminders of the boy who wanted to see the world, who cast aside the warm blankets of his bed to set out in the early morning darkness, cold and afraid, but eager to go.

This was my first "expedition." A lifetime of expeditions, to some seventy countries, have since come and gone, but that first trip — the boy on the bike — remains the most memorable. It was the underpinning, the motivating force, for all that followed.

In 1961, barely eighteen, I made a journey of some 3,000 miles around the U.S., Mexico, and Canada in a VW camper. My fellow adventurer was my best friend, Woodie Hartman. We had met in Connecticut as neighbors when we were thirteen. Turned out our interests meshed and our friendship had deepened over the years. The trip would be the first of its kind for both of us.

I remember vividly our first lunch, a simple meal of pea soup, French bread, and cheese which we ate on a curb in our torn jeans, T-shirts, and bare feet. We imagined ourselves "dharma bums," convinced all things were possible. We drank a toast to the open road. In the distance green corn shimmered under an azure sky. All the mornings of the world rolled out before us. We were artless, carefree, undaunted.

So captivating was the two-month trip with its exotic landscapes and equally exotic people that, two years later, we decided to do it again. This time we added more back roads, more remote public lands, and more towns on the edge of nowhere. But halfway through our travels, somewhere near Bisbee, Arizona, I realized I needed to see the world through my own eyes alone. Woodie was looking to pursue his interests in natural history and I needed more interaction with people. Neither of us wanted to be an impediment to the other. We parted with warm blessings, anticipating a reunion rich with tales to tell.

I boarded a bus bound for Mexico and eased myself into the seat opposite the driver. The window was clean, the view expansive. With the motor idling and other passengers boarding, it dawned on me, as I looked out at the desert and vast sky and straight road south, that I could be anyone I wanted to be. At that moment, I sensed that my life had taken an irreversible turn. Away from family and friends, navigating my own course — now, at last, I could call my life "mine." I began to picture villages on the horizon where grandfathers would welcome me and hardscrabble farmers would break bread with me. I envisioned shamans and vagabonds, mystics and outcasts around the next bend in the road. For the first time I was certain of my future and certain of myself. A life of travel merged with my dreams that hot morning as the bus headed south to the Mexican border.

A day later, I stepped off in a village called Creel in the State of Chihuahua. Creel was a logging town high in the Tarahumara Mountains. It seemed charged with energy and mystery. Indians in white tunics and red sashes were gathered in small groups around the plaza. Mestizo farmers came through town, their horses and burros loaded with produce. The sweet smell of piñon smoke hung in the air. I spent the first night sleeping with locals in a railroad dormitory whose amenities consisted of a porcelain washbasin and pitcher, a kerosene lamp, and a privy. The aroma of a simmering meal filtered into the hallway. Women laughed, old men told jokes, and teenage boys strummed guitars and sang haunting love songs. All this for a dollar a night. I was finally home!

A few years later, I had finished college and moved to Vermont where I married and fathered a son. I worked fourteen years for the state, first as a schoolteacher, then as deputy director of the Vermont Historical Society. It was there that I fell in love with black and white documentary photography and oral history. Whenever I felt overwhelmed by desk work, I would check out of the office with a couple of cameras and a tape recorder to visit loggers, blacksmiths, dairy farmers, back-to-the-landers, former moonshiners and rum-runners, anyone who smacked of earthiness and old-timey ways. I realized that interviewing and photographing such characters was what I wanted to do with my life.

During this period I got divorced and raised my son, Taylor, for four years. In 1978 he went to live with his mother. This freed me to sell my house, resign from my job, and devote myself entirely to travel and photography. In 1979 I bought an old VW camper and decorated it with flower decals and rainbows. I discarded the back seats and in their place installed a comfy bed and cooking area. A sturdy roof rack allowed me to carry my bicycle and kayak. It was, I must admit, a *bona fide* "hippie mobile."

My experience in Vermont had taught me that my sights were set on country folk: in particular, anachronisms, oddities, those marginalized by the modern world. I would now broaden my scope to embrace such types across the continent — and, eventually, around the globe.

I ask myself why I am drawn to throwbacks, to the salt of the earth, to the poor and the downtrodden? Why do I enjoy the company of such people? Why, among my subjects, are there no bankers, no businessmen, no merchants, no city dwellers, no suburbanites, no one fashionable or affluent? *Especially* since I am a college graduate myself and come from wealth, inheriting the means that has made possible my travels.

White-collared professionals, after all, struggle to make ends meet, struggle to raise families, struggle with relationships and personal issues — no different from the soiled and sweat-drenched characters that people my photos. Why then am I not drawn to persons of my own ilk? Why do I feel so little affinity with them? Indeed, I seek to photograph and associate with those who represent the opposite of refinement and education, the opposite, that is, of my heritage and culture.

The answer, no doubt, has deep and complex roots, best not left to an amateur like me. But to satisfy my own curiosity, I have come up with the following explanation. For someone who is college educated, I am astonishingly unschooled, with an attention deficit more typical of children. I am fully aware of my intellectual shortfalls and because of them find official functions and dinner parties with sophisticated people intimidating. The sharper the repartee at such gatherings — the wittier the conversation, the more clever the insights — the greater my discomfort. To compensate, I take refuge with unassuming people. It is with them, plainly, that I find my delight and identity.

There is, of course, more to it than the self-consciousness and insecurity I feel in the presence of my peers. I look at polite society and I see a world that is both isolated and insulated from the down-to-earth people I hold so dear. The material comforts of the white-collar world come at the expense of the persons in my photographs — potato diggers, goatherds, coffee pickers, scythers of hay, hired hands — who make luxury and leisure possible, yet have time for neither themselves. I find polite society to be a world sustained by posing, posturing, pompousness, and pretense; by defenses polished and subtle; by hypocrisy honed to an art. In contrast, the earthy provincials who populate so many of my photographs — my adopted "family" — strike me as guileless, grounded, forthright, innocent, spontaneous, authentic.

Sandwiched between the portraits of hunters, gatherers, nomads, "old fashioned" farmers, grizzled elders, and glowing youth — indigent and indigenous people for the most part — you will find an occasional face that registers emptiness or befuddlement, the product of a brain injury or genetic defect. I go out of my way to cultivate friendships with such "cognitively challenged" people. Fooling around in their company is the only time I feel completely at ease. Somehow they manage to erase every shred of self-consciousness in me. Their utter lack of sophistication, their childishness, disarms and intoxicates me. Must be that their simple mindedness mirrors my own. Little wonder, then, that I find them magnetic and actively seek them out stocking shelves in supermarkets or cleaning public toilets. The moment we begin a conversation, I sense an immediate connection. The language they speak may be barely intelligible, but it is always without premeditation and to the point. We are soon joshing and enjoying a meeting of minds unlike anything I've ever known except with young children.

There is one other thread woven through my life and photos that has had as great an influence on me as the colorful curiosities and relics that comprise the bulk of this book. I am referring to my spiritual quest and the long and venerable list of teachers who have guided me. I have been a "spiritual seeker" since my eary twenties when someone introduced me to Ram Dass's *Be Here Now*. At one point or another, in my search for inner peace and self-knowledge, I have turned to gurus, roshis, rinpoches, monks, channelers, dream analysts, visionaries, shamans and psychotherapists. I have been to countless retreats and have practiced everything from meditation, deep breathing, yoga, and rebirthing to chanting, visualizations, prostrations, and "kirtan" dancing. Most of my teachers have been Buddhists, but I am impressed by the writings of mystics, past and present, from all religious traditions. I have sat at the feet of Native American holy men, of psychiatrists, of the Dalai Lama, even of an "awakened" Vermont carpenter. I must confess that many of the more profound and subtle elements of their teachings have gone in one ear and out the other, and, in moments of doubt, I wonder if all the time and money spent shopping around the spiritual marketplace has been worth it. What do I have to show for it? What insights have I gained? What depths of self-knowledge have I plumbed? What,

in the end, have the great masters and my various "practices" taught me that I haven't learned, say, from Paul, the shelf-stocker with Down syndrome at Price Chopper or Loyda and Beti, the beaming young sisters of my Mayan neighbors in Guatemala. If the purpose of spiritual inquiry is — depending on which of my teachers you ask — to find one's soul, to forget the self, to live in the present, or to intuit union with the cosmos, then innocents, from young children to befuddled illiterates, have taken me closer to these objectives than have any of my revered masters. Playing "This Little Piggy Went to Market" with Tibetan orphans in the Himalayas means as much to me as reciting mantras with hundreds of fellow seekers aspiring to enlightenment at some mammoth international gathering. And I'll be damned if drinking whiskey with an old weather-beaten drover in a cellar hole in the Outer Hebrides doesn't take me as close to the "truth" as sitting on a cushion in a zendo for a month.

Friends often ask me how do you choose your subjects and how do you get them to "open up" so unselfconsciously? All I can say is that I've trained my eye and trust my intuition to pick, in a sea of a thousand faces, the ones that hold the promise of *losing my self in*. Of tapping my own authenticity? Am I looking for my own innocence in the faces of my subjects?

I have no formula, no "line," when I approach a prospective subject. Quite the opposite, I am usually nervous and embarrassed, fumble and falter most unprofessionally. Add to that a dose of awkward foolishness, and as best as I can judge, I come across, not as an aloof artist but as a bungling loopy adolescent. Maybe the secret lies in that I do not look upon my "people" as photographic objects but as brethren. I identify, *genuinely identify* with them, which allows me, apparently, to break through. We end up putting each other at ease and embracing in trust.

Frank, Loyda, Donald John, Alvaro, Mr. Ryan, Marie Lorette — they are my family now. They give me something my own blood relatives cannot, something fresh, immediate, accepting, nonjudgmental. And they connect me in a way neither spiritual insights nor my own class and culture can. It is a connection my childish antics and lack of intellect seems to encourage.

These, then, are my *people* — disheveled and dirty, crazed and cherubic, dark and radiant, lost and found — and this is my tribute to them, a thank-you note, a way of repaying them for putting me in touch with my heart.

May you, too, lose your self in their faces!

— Ethan Hubbard, July, 2011

Note: The photographs in this book were taken between 1968 and 2011. Many of these images have appeared in several of my previous books: *Vermont: Light upon the Mountains* (1977), *Good Folks, Good Country* (1979), *First Light* (1986), *Journey to Ollantaytambo* (1990), *Salt Pork & Apple Pie* (2004), *Grandfather's Gift* (2007), and *Thirty Below Zero* (2009).

Vermont, USA

The first time I met Harry Smith, he was standing in the manger of a barn prying out his last tooth with the claw of a hammer, instantly endearing himself to me. In short order he became my best friend and adoptive father.

In 1969, having lost my wife, son, and home in divorce, I erected a tipi on Harry's land in Waitsfield. Christmas came that year and with it a dread that bit to the bone. I was lost, awash in self-pity. Over a breakfast of oatmeal and toast in his old-fashioned kitchen on Christmas morn, Harry suggested that I hike up nearby Bald Mountain to relieve my anxiety. An hour later I was on the summit where I proceeded to celebrate my own Christmas with prayers, a roaring fire, hot soup, and a long meditation. The surrounding world of valleys and mountains, blue skies and wispy clouds, filled my heart.

Feeling reaffirmed, I skipped down the backside of the mountain, flinging bread crusts from a gunnysack Harry had given me — to feed the hungry winter birds. Near the bottom I halted at the edge of a field and placed my hands in prayer. Suddenly, from a few hundred yards away, a huge ball of red-orange light came charging fast as a speeding car across the snow, smacked me at my ankles, then rolled up my body and into my face. I fell to the ground unconscious. When I came to, I rose bewildered, crying and laughing, crying and laughing.

Back at Harry's, he was waiting for me and, when I was finally able to catch my breath, I told him what had happened. "Hell," he said, "I seen that light many times, mostly coming back from milking at night. It's a good sign, Hubbard. It means angels is telling you, 'Don't you never let anyone steal your soul again.' Couldn't you hear 'em?"

Courtesy of Emily Von Trapp

Vermont, USA

One hot summer night I slept under the stars on the summit of Hunger Mountain. I was secretly hoping to be awakened by a space ship manned by friendly aliens sent to impart celestial knowledge. Instead, the only creature I encountered was a hare that jumped on my belly and made me scream. The following day I hiked down to my friends, the Chases, a family of four eking out a living on their hardscrabble farm. They *had* seen space aliens. I queried them about the incident. Elroy, the older son, piped up from a noon meal of biscuits and bacon drippings, "We seen a spaceship in our orchard last year about this time. Two aliens got out and they was armed with rifles. Ain't that right, Ma?"

I tented that night among the apple trees hoping aliens would land beside me. Around midnight I went out to pee, nervously expectant. It was a moonlit night with heavy ground fog, made yet eerier by the dripping boughs. Sensing something behind me, I turned on my heels and there, staring me in the face — ghostly, grinning, wild-eyed in the pale light — were brothers Elroy and Eugene. My heart stopped as I jumped backwards.

"Seen any of 'em yet, Ethan?" Eugene asked as I regained my composure. After they left, I went back to bed and tried to sleep, but couldn't shake the thought that perhaps I was years too late and that aliens had indeed slipped under the radar and made landfall right here.

Come to think of it, Elroy and Eugene could be them!

Vermont, USA

In January of 1970 I moved from Waitsfield to Craftsbury in the Northeast Kingdom — in part because I was drawn to the old-timey customs that persisted there. I purchased an eighteen-acre hillside plot from a farmer. The land looked to the west, to sunsets on Mount Mansfield and the Lowell Range. Quebec was a mere twenty miles to the north.

I cut poles and, with the help of friends, erected a white canvas tipi with black bear claws imprinted along the bottom. Taylor, my son of five, helped commemorate the event by spending the first night inside with me. We slept in thick sleeping bags upon hay beside the fire pit. I lived alone in this tipi for the next nine months, until my new house was completed in October.

Many of Craftsbury's farms were owned and operated by Franco-Americans. Most older folks in town still spoke "Québécois." One of the largest French families up my way were the Patoines: fifteen siblings and their parents. (Their mother, Rosa, eventually lived to her 101st birthday.) This portrait of three strapping Patoine brothers was made at the Lumberjack Festival in Barton where they were participants.

I saw Frank the other day and asked him if he had any good stories. "Why shore," he said. "I got this old mule, see. Had him for a century or more, seems. Work with him plowin' some and skiddin'. Always have to be careful with him, though. Never can fully trust a mule. Like, one afternoon I went out to the field to scatter some hay for him. Oh, I'd say he was a good fifteen feet from me, looked happy enough and all. The next thing I knew my thigh was on fire with pain 'cause that son of a gun lunged backwards across them fifteen feet and nailed me good. I mean NAILED ME GOOD, mister man, with his hind foot. I was sore for a week. I've still got the bastard, though… must be 'cause I'm just as stubborn and ornery as him!"

Vermont, USA

Florence Hacon of Craftsbury never spoke more than a handful of words.

After she had walked three miles to church one morning — at 10° below zero — I asked her, "How was your walk, Florence?" "Oh, t'weren't too bad," she said vacantly.

No emotion, no follow through, no engagement. Her apparent emptiness intrigued me and drove me to know more about her. Did she enjoy her long forays along the Creek Road in sun, rain, or snow? Was she lonely or depressed? Happy and fulfilled? Did she crave friends, amusements? Did she even care about such things? What, if anything, did she feel? Alas, she would never talk about such matters and remained an utter mystery. "Oh, I dunno," she'd reply typically.

I noticed, however, that, like a savant, there were two subjects Florence was fixated upon and would routinely bring up out of the blue: the names and birthdays of acquaintances.

One day I was thrilled to see her approaching me along a steep hill, her squat body walking determinedly in the purple haze of a summer's sunset. I felt as if I was encountering a rare bird. As we passed on the road, I heard her say to herself, "Ethan Hubbard, December 6th, 1941."

Vermont, USA

Romeo Beaudry, Franco-Vermonter, once told me that he put up two cords of unsplit logs in a single day with only a double-bitted axe. Snow is piled high against the north side of his house and a chill wind is rattling the windowpanes when I come to see him one bright winter's day in Albany. Cold light pours in upon the man, luminously, like a painting by Rembrandt. A North Country still life.

Romeo takes me to inspect his handiwork. As we walk through deep drifts, I can smell him, his sweat, the chain saw oil and gas on his trousers, the sawdust clinging to his woolens. When we come to a clearing, we are greeted by an amphitheater of spruce and pine pulpwood, stacked tall as a man's chest. Blinding sunlight bathes the clearing, illuminating one month's work.

Back at his house, Romeo offers neither tea nor coffee, only himself. I must accept the silence surrounding him. He sits and stares out the window and waits for me to ask him logging questions. His frugality with words seems to say, "You've seen what I can do. Surely that's good 'nuff."

Vermont, USA

Forest Belknap was an ox of a man who once lifted a thousand pounds to his knees. He was a logger by profession, but he made ends meet by being a jack-of-all-trades. I came to know and love him when, as a neighbor, he volunteered one day to muck out my barn.

Forest was "the Dump Master" of Craftsbury, a position of status or ill repute, depending on whom you talked to. I took my garbage every Saturday just so I could visit with my friend. On winter afternoons, Forest could be found drunk in his walnut-sized shack at the dump, peering out of the small window and collecting fees.

Forest always greeted me as if I were the King of Norway, pulling me into his hovel with strong hands and cracking open a beer for me. It was always warm inside and the odors of Forest intense: coagulated chewing tobacco on his face and neck, old urine-soaked trousers, shirts stinking of dump debris, stale beer reeking from the man. Still, it awed me to be in his presence, to feel his fatherly tenderness. He always made me feel special and never missed a chance to bequeath me a present — a broken "plumber's friend," a dirty spatula, frozen vice grips, a plastic owl missing both its feet.

The "Pete and Repeat" family prepare for winter. Vermont

Cy McCoy, teamster. Vermont

Vermont, USA

When I came upon the old man, he was stashing his butter and cream in a well to keep it cool. I stopped and chatted with him in the noon heat. He had a thick accent and an unusual, "old-fashioned" way of standing and gesturing, a nineteenth century man exiled in the twentieth century. This was Theron Boyd.

When not tending his gardens, milking his five cows, or scything his meadows to gather loose hay for winter forage, Theron dug graves in his hometown of Quechee.

One day Theron invited me in for dinner. He carefully prepared a meal of cold tongue, beet greens, new potatoes in milk gravy, and a drink of "switchel" (water spiked with vinegar and molasses or maple syrup). While we ate, Theron talked about the developers and real estate agents who were trying to pry him off his farm for a "second home" complex they wanted to build.

He looked at me with one eyebrow raised so high it nearly reached his hairline. "Why, we never pulled them kind of shenanigans back when my father and grandfather were alive. Them kind of corporation liars and scoundrels just weren't 'round when I was young. But I'll tell you one thing, I'll never sell to them. Never! This is my home and these are my meadows. I know just how the moon comes up through them maples. Nobody's going to take that from me."

Vermont, USA

Tenney Call lived with his wife and son in a shed in West Brookfield. Despite severe poverty, constant pain throughout his body, a sick wife and a handicapped son, Tenney held tightly to a philosophy of hope, strength, and kindness.

Tenney and his son, Oakley, did their laundry every Wednesday in Montpelier, hitching a ride into town with a neighbor. From my office window I would see them in summer heat or winter cold as they pulled their old hand cart, loaded with clothes, to and from the laundromat. They were often taunted by local teenagers who would snatch Oakley's hat and keep it from him. Oakley would lunge at them in awkward attempts to retrieve it. I would go out and chase the boys away, get the hat, dust it off, and return it to Oakley, who would be teary-eyed but smiling.

Sometimes I invited myself to have lunch with them. We would eat together in the, boiler room of my building where they could be found waiting for their evening ride home. Next to the warm pipes in the bowels of the building, they shared their applesauce and graham crackers, and I would divide whatever I had brought along. Sometimes Tenney would read one or two of his poems, the hissing pipes nearly drowning out his lines. His words of loving-kindness for his sick wife, Evelyn, and toward his handicapped son — toward all of humanity really — touched me deeply. His poems often talked about the small, simple gifts of Nature; they spoke of faith and inspiration, transcendence over grief and despair. True solace, they were.

Vermont, USA

Ann Burke never doubted that life was beneficent. An aura of abundance surrounded her. She and her husband farmed. Their beloved Harvest Hill was a poignant anomaly; it was the last farm in the town of Berlin. Office buildings, a hospital, a school, a shopping mall, an airport, and new homes had slowly surrounded it. Like the children's story in which the old couple's farmhouse is swallowed up by skyscrapers, the modern world had encircled the Burkes. But it didn't bother Ann in the least.

As I took a photo of Ann in her barn, a shaft of light slid through a crack and spread across her face. With her calf beside her, the entire world seemed to coalesce about her in radiance.

Vermont, USA

One bitter March day I accompanied Ray Burke out to his "Sweet Tooth Inn" (the sugar house) to watch him boil sap. Snow during the night had obliterated the path through the field, making walking difficult. Ray is blind, but when I took his arm to help him, he politely declined my offer. He marched along grinning and humming a Hank Williams tune. When I am with Ray, I often feel that he is the one taking care of me.

Blindness seems to be the last thing on Ray's mind. He plows through life with assurance and competence. As a father, husband, farmer, logger, mechanic, saxophonist, and radio dispatcher for the State Highway Department, one is quick to disbelieve that he is "handicapped." For years, blind, Ray hitchhiked the two miles to his State job.

The Burkes recently purchased 30 acres of land adjoining their farm in Berlin. Soon after, I stopped to see Ray but couldn't find him in the house or barn. Hearing the whine of a chain saw, I followed the noise out to the new acreage. There, amid a thick stand of cedar and pine, was Ray — using his chain saw to cut down trees for fence posts! "First I feel the girth of the tree, then start up my saw, come down to the base, and cut her down. It's slow work, but what the heck. I ain't in no rush. I'm just happy to be alive."

Vermont, USA

Josephine Young, 91, lived in Craftsbury on the Creek Road with her daughter, Viola. She spent her summers sitting in a rocking chair on the front porch watching barn swallows sail in the sky. She would rock or just sit still, the summer winds blowing her beautiful white hair in wisps about the deep lines of her face. She was only vaguely present; her mind had long since gone off "somewhere else."

Occasionally she would get up from her rocker, go to her room, pack a small valise with clothing, comb and brush, then depart north on the road. She would always shamble off in the same direction, head held upright despite the heat, advancing slowly toward her old home place on a distant hillside. "I'm going home now. That's where I'm going. I'm going home."

Viola would go after her. She never tried to dissuade her mother, just kept an eye on her so she wouldn't get lost. Josephine rarely went far. A few hundred yards seemed to satisfy her need to emigrate. Then Josephine would reconsider and shuffle back to the house with her daughter.

Vermont, USA

In the summer of her fiftieth year — with lumber donated by a local sawmill and a crew of four gay friends — Duffy Clearwaters built herself a shanty.

She chose a location exactly four feet from a tumbling brook whose hisses and gurgles, she knew, would provide her daily therapy.

Her dooryard soon turned into a maze of cast-off furniture, windsocks, wind chimes, rusty wall hangings, bird feeders, pennants, and raised garden beds. With a clutch of brown hens foraging at her feet, she became the neighborhood's anomaly: a fiercely liberal homesteading "daughter of Lesbos."

Duffy lived peacefully beside the stream for five years. Then one winter's night, in the midst of a January thaw, she awoke to the din of ice chunks bouncing off rocks and trees. An icy "flash flood" had already risen to her cabin's footings.

"I grabbed my dog, Feather, and made a dash to higher ground." Out of breath on the road, she muttered, "Sonofabitch, you'd think I intentionally chose a flood zone! But if I hadn't, then I wouldn't have had five years of stream music playing on my heart strings."

Vermont, USA

Ernie Wheeler lived with his mother on the old home place. He was a throwback to the days when people came to town on horse-drawn wagons and sleighs. Ernie and "Flossie," his Morgan mare, made the trip to Plainfield in half an hour. They returned with staples like flour, tea, soap, and kerosene for lamps.

Just up the road from Plainfield was Goddard, a radical liberal arts college with an enrollment, in 1968, of some 1200 students who were attracted by courses that ranged from "social anarchism" to "basket weaving." Most of the students looked like they had been recruited by Jerry Rubin from the Haight-Ashbury district of San Francisco.

To these hippies Ernie Wheeler seemed a kind of living fossil, an animatronic museum specimen escaped from a diorama in the anthropology wing. Or perhaps he'd just stepped out of central casting for *Birth of a Nation*. The Age of Aquarius meets Ethan Frome.

Ernie became something of a small town star. "Didja see Ernie today?" a pretty gal with a Brooklyn accent asked her friend at Mae's Gas and Groceries. "He's so goddam cute I can't stand it."

One warm spring day I saw Flossie and the buckboard at the curb by the hardware store. Surrounding Ernie on the wagon were five dreamy hippie chicks. Ernie looked like the proverbial cat who had just swallowed a canary — in this case, five canaries.

36

Vermont, USA

Francese Cochran loves dancing. "The faster the music, the better I like it. Polkas are a favorite of mine, whirling around the dance floor as if I was a princess living in a dream."

After her husband died in 1975, she began a pastime she pursues to this day. Francese, now 88, visits nursing homes to dance with the residents.

"I'll drive myself over to the Maple Lane Nursing Home in Barton, say, or over to Union House in Glover, and just barge right in, go up to folks just sitting around doing nothing, waiting … for what to happen? I get the staff to put on a jazzy record, then drag an old man out of his chair. If he sputters and groans and says he's too old to dance, I pull his ear and yank him to his feet. I'll dance with women too, doesn't make any difference to me. Whoever's my partner, I'll have 'em laughing soon enough."

When I ask Francese why she does it, she smiles in reply, "Keeps you young!"

Vermont, USA

Glen Duger (left) was the unofficial patriarch of tiny West Woodbury. He had built his tar paper shack up against a cliff to keep the northwest winds from blasting through the wide open cracks in the chinks. "Some frigid nights," Glen told me, "when the stove won't draw and my wood ain't burnin' worth shit, I'll go to the barn and bed down in between two cows to save my ass."

One hellish day in January, things went horribly awry for Glen. "Jesum, I bet the temperature was close to 30° below zero! I started drinkin' early on to get my blood circulatin', but the cold beat me down. By sundown I was shiverin' so bad that my teeth played music. Only thing to do, git to the barn and find some warmth with the cows."

During the night, the horse blanket that Glen threw over himself slipped off one foot. "Come dawn, I realized the toes on that foot was froze." He lost those toes to surgery but was soon back on his feet no worse for wear.

The next summer I ran into Glen. "I ain't puttin' up with none of that freezin' shit this winter, and I ain't beddin' down with them cows no more," he exclaimed. "I'm gonna hitch me up an electric blanket to a Delco battery."

"Codfish" Clough at the fiddle contest. Vermont

Wade and Maxwell Maxham, Connecticut River farmers. Vermont

Maine, USA

Early one fall I drove to Maine to be with my friends, John and Ellen Gawler. They are organic farmers, travelers, and musicians. They introduced me to The Common Ground Fair in Litchfield, a three-day event showcasing organic agriculture, traditional crafts, and folk music. I thrilled to an afternoon concert that my raggle-taggle friends performed before an audience of fellow back-to-the-landers. But for me the crowning jewel of the fair was an impromptu event observed by a handful of sleepy fairgoers wending their way back to their cars at day's end: John and Ellen playing fiddle and banjo under a street lamp, as couples waltzed slowly, dreamily to their music in the misty night air.

Maine, USA

Bob Wag, trapper, and Woodie Hartman, conservationist, reunite at the Common Ground Fair. Woodie (right) is into saving animals, refining his diet, jogging, and studying Zen. "Old Wag," on the other hand, kills animals, thrives on cigarettes and Hostess Twinkies, jogs only to get a beer out of the frig, and has never heard of Zen.

Obviously, it hasn't affected their friendship.

47

Maine, USA

Andrew Dana is a Passamaquoddy Indian living on tribal lands near Peter Dana Point, "Downeast." In a bog below his cabin he runs a trap line where he snares beavers for their pelts. Andrew is deaf and mute, as is his girlfriend who often traps with him.

The afternoon I visited the couple, snow squalls barreled across the low-lying swale beclouding the landscape. All seemed ethereal, the spruce and cedars along the shore appearing and disappearing.

As the couple was conversing in sign language near a trap, a strong gust of wind-born snow obliterated them. When the wind calmed and visibility improved, their outlines reappeared like a sepia image from a centuries-old collection by Edward Curtis.

As I peered from an evergreen thicket, I imagined Andrew and his girlfriend to be "Old Ones," ancient people of the north, down from Siberia and the Bering Land Bridge 20,000 years ago, just as the last continental glacier melted away.

First on the land.

South Carolina, USA

Having saved some precious vacation days from my work at the Vermont Historical Society, I head south in my bus to experience the coming of spring in Fort Motte. Upon arrival, I am caught by a violent storm and take refuge in the parking lot of Mount Pleasant Baptist Church.

In the morning after breakfast, I rummage for a coat and tie and a clean pair of slacks in order to attend the day's service. Eddie Brown and his three brothers, all Deacons of the church, warmly welcome me. They ask if I will witness to the Lord from the pulpit, and hesitantly, I agree. When the time comes, the pastor nods to me and I walk self-consciously to the front to say a few words about Jesus. I speak briefly about my own thirst for the words of the great teacher, praising his courage, patience, forgiveness, and especially his love toward enemies.

I have with me Doris Ulman's *Former Slaves of the Lang Syne Plantation* which was located here in Fort Motte. I suspect that some of the congregation have great-grandparents and other relatives portrayed among its fine photographs. Outside, after the service, I produce the book and, sure enough, some four dozen church members are ecstatic to find long lost relations among its photos. "Why there's Great Aunt Rose! And look here, that's got to be Old Silas! Mercy sakes, isn't that Pearly Mae's gramma, Bessie?

Mother and child. "Not a stick of wood left to warm the house today." Georgia

Johnny Dillard. "It's a hazard to be born poor." Mississippi

South Carolina, USA

I took the mail boat from Savanna, Georgia, to tiny Daufuskie Island, home to a small population of blacks and not a single automobile. I disembarked at the jetty, swung my backpack onto my shoulders, and began walking slowly to nowhere in particular, happy to be under canopies of swamp cyprus, pine, and live oaks draped with Spanish moss.

I heard the sound of metal wheels and hoof beats on the dirt track behind me. My heart quickened when a large hand, big as a ham hock, reached down from a wagon and offered to hoist me up. "Come on up, son, I'll show you the island."

His name was James Williams and he eventually brought me to his little cabin in the piney woods. He told me I could pitch my tent next to it.

After dinner with James, I walked back to the jetty to the pay phone to call my parents. My father answered and as usual was gruff and dismissive. "Dad, Dad, you wouldn't believe the luck I had today finding a man who had a wagon pulled by a bull! Dad, it would have been as if Queen Elizabeth had picked you up in her Rolls Royce. Dad? Dad? Are you there, Dad?"

Lester and Jick Taylor. "Taylors were the first ranchers in these mountains." Utah

Ben Washington. "No car for me. Just me and my little red mules." Mississippi

North Carolina, USA

I envy most of the hermits I have met: how they pretty much do whatever they want whenever they want.

At the Hayesville General Store, the proprietor told me about Otis Beech who lived up in a hollow beneath the Blue Ridge Mountains. He said the Beeches had been here since Revolutionary times. Said Otis lived alone, was odd but not crazy.

Otis was walking in circles in the driveway when I pulled in. At first, he paid no attention to me and continued to circle. After an uncomfortably long time, he detoured toward me but swerved away at the last minute and began talking in a twang to his three hound dogs.

He walked toward his dilapidated house, dogs in tow, still paying me no mind. I followed him into what I guess could be called a living room. Nervous chickens with no neck feathers came and went through massive holes in the floor. Otis sat in a sorry looking recliner that was leaking stuffing. He was making noises like the chickens.

To my surprise, he ate the hippie fare I served him from my van: steamed bulgur, greens, coarse bread and sweet chai. He barely spoke, though I made every effort to engage him in conversation. When through with his food, he burped twice, wiped his chin on his sleeve, and put my wooden bowl in the dirt where his dogs cleaned it up.

He said I could spend the night in his driveway. In the morning he surprised me with a breakfast that turned out to be most excellent: toast with home-grown comb honey, grits with sorghum molasses, and strong coffee in the dirtiest cup I had ever seen. As I was leaving, he chirped, "Come again, Mr. Ethan, if ever down this way. I liked meeting you."

You just never know!

Mississippi, USA

I poked around the Deep South in Oxford County, spending most of my time with old black men who owned mules. There's something I find irresistible about old men and mules, and Ed Couch was a mule man to the bone.

"I never drove a car! Dis here is my Jo. She my transportation. I got her when she be just six months, now she thirty. Named her after my neighbor's wife. Taught her everything she know, how to plow and harrow de corn and de cotton."

Mister Ed Couch and I became fast friends, and in the cool of the piney woods he talked about his life as a sharecropper. When I asked about the Klan and Jim Crow, he opened right up. "It's all still round here, never gonna go away complete. So I minds my manners, stay low. But I gots my dreams just like everybody. I dreams to go to de movies in town, eat at Woolworth's, use de rest rooms, drink from de fountains. Be equal like Medgar tryin' to be. Maybe join in wid dem Masons."

On my last evening in Abbeville, I drove once more to Mister Couch's house to say goodbye. He was not home. Passing an old abandoned building down the road, I spied lamp light and men in suits moving about the upstairs. I thought I detected the silhouette of Mister Couch. I hung around a few minutes, then drove back to my host family, the owners of Jimmy's Café. Over milkshakes and burgers with Jimmy, he explained what I had just seen. "You were right, Ethan. You saw Ed Couch up there with his men-folk neighbors. They were having their own 'Masonic Order' meeting. They're not permitted to join the real Masons, but *in their imagination* they belong. They've been holding meetings in that old slaughterhouse for over five years now, and nobody, thank God, has thrown them out."

Mississippi, USA

It was 1968 and my presence in Oxford County didn't go unnoticed. I was being watched. One afternoon as I was reading in my van on a dirt road, two white men drove up slowly, got out, and approached me. They seemed friendly enough and invited me up to their trailer to drink a little whiskey. I didn't dare say no and followed them in my van.

It didn't take but a minute for the Rakestraw brothers to begin grilling me on what I was doing here. I told them I was spending time with black men and their mules. At once the air in the trailer turned icy.

Stupidly, I wouldn't back down and rose to the defense of African Americans. I told them my mother had marched with Ralph Abernathy and I praised the decision to admit James Meredith to Ole Miss. No surprise, things quickly went from bad to nasty. The brothers came up to me, shoving and jostling me, swearing that I was as ignorant and dangerous as the Blacks. Sensing real trouble, I bolted out the door and ran to my van. I gunned it all the way to Jimmy's Café, hoping to find refuge there.

I was telling my story to Jimmy and his parents at the counter when the door blasted open and in stormed the fuming Rakestraws. "Where's that nigger lover?" the big one snarled. "Better get your white ass back to VER-mont or you're asking for big trouble." I quaked on my stool. But Jimmy would have none of it, stepped up to pinch hit for me, calmed the brothers down, told them to go home and cool off.

"Funny thing," Jimmy said to me later, "those brothers saved my life last year when my boat capsized. I don't know how to swim. The two of them swam out in the snake-infested lake to rescue me. You just never know what twists and turns life's gonna take, do you?"

Virginia, USA

With help from his manager blind Gospel singer, Daniel Womack, carefully descended the stairs from the stage in the Roanoke revival tent. He stood motionless on the lawn until a few people came up and spoke to him.

I patiently waited my turn, then went to him. Feeling my presence, he extended his immense hand and shook mine, though in truth it was less a "shake" than his hand enfolding and penetrating mine. For the several sweet minutes that ensued, we did not let go of one another.

"My mother and father were "Gospel Jubilee" singers and they raised me up to carry on the tradition of singing the Lord's praises. I must always remain meek so the Lord can work through me. I need to remain humble, a humble servant of God."

I was reluctant to let go of his hand as I fumbled to tell him how good it was to have made his acquaintance, how I would try to see him again, but holding his hand spoke more than a thousand of my faltering words.

Art Storley. "I was raised up on 'kitchen junkets'." North Dakota

Kenny Runion. "Them hippie-folks love to buy my hand-fashioned wood jewelry." Georgia

Texas, USA

From the curb in my bus I spied an old cowboy dining at a Fort Stockton café. He was eating chicken wings with his fingers. I sat behind the wheel, motor shut down, and wondered how I was going to pull off meeting him, which I knew I had to do. To break the ice with him, however, I was wearing the absolutely "wrongest" attire: gauzy see-through yoga pants and shirt, sandals with no socks, ankle bracelets of pink and blue, a necklace of red coral and turquoise stones ... and my hair was way too long. But I was determined, so I rummaged in the bus for the "right" clothes and ended up putting on boots, jeans, a blue canvas shirt, bandana, and straw hat. I sauntered into the café, trying desperately to act like a veteran cowboy, and sat down at a table a bare two feet from my target.

Lo, within minutes — after I hesitatingly opened with 'How 'bout them Houston Oilers?" — Morris Hart was offering me his unfinished plate of chicken wings, sweetened with stories of his cattle ranch forty miles down the highway. And ... get this ... did I want to see it? *Did I want to see it?!*

I ended up spending the weekend with Morris. We strung fencing, drove cattle, and irrigated fields — all the while nipping at his bottle of Wild Turkey. He invited me to watch the Super Bowl with him at a honky-tonk down the road. I thought I had died and gone to heaven when the bouncer didn't blink twice as he greeted us with a polite western benediction: "Looks like you two cowpokes have been workin' hard. Come on in and wet your whistles."

Texas, USA

I love this picture of a boy roping a calf along the Rio Grande.

Mountains of Mexico in distance.
     Lariat hissing.
     Boot heel poised,
planting toes to leverage throwing arm.
     Fingers and thumb release.
Air is split in two by flight of stiff sisal.

For the boy, there is only this moment,
     lasso and calf under a hot sun.

Nebraska, USA

In 1968 I stopped at Phil Connaughton's garage to get a leaking tire fixed. I was his first customer that morning. He told me in a twangy Nebraska accent, "First thing I do is unlock the place and feed my twelve cats on the steps. Then I put my feet up on the desk and wait for customers like you."

Phil started his tire business back in 1926. He ran an old-fashioned operation where town kids could get free tube patches for their bike tires and a grown-up who'd listen to their troubles, a place you'd find a hand-written note on the door saying, "Down at the café for coffee — come join me." Phil was the type of guy who would give you five stamped postcards from his old roll-top desk and say, "Drop me a line from time to time, I'd enjoy hearing about your travels."

Twenty years later I rolled into Wisner to see if Phil was still alive, let alone in business. I arrived at 7:00 A.M. and waited. He soon appeared — and remembered me! We laughed and carried on. Then he got down to business. First, he unlocked the door, then went about feeding his cats. Done with that, he went into his office and put his feet on the desk. With his hands behind his head, he looked out the window and waited for customers.

"How's business?" I asked him. "Oh, hell, Ethan, I'm not in business any more. Retired years ago. Come in every day though. Got to have my routine. Everything's the same except I don't have any tires to sell. Just pretend that I do. Takes the edge off growing old and heading to the grave, dontcha think?"

Arizona, USA

I met two old Tohono O'Odham Indians, Hoosie and Laura, living in a compound in the Sonora Desert. Born near the turn of the century in a cave in the mountains, they were still living traditional lives much as their people always have.

Hoosie reminded me of Ishi, a Stone Age Indian who walked out of the mountains of northern California and surrendered to the modern world in 1911. Hoosie was silent and secretive, and although I spent a full week with him, I cannot say I came to understand him in the least. He spoke no English and rarely, if ever, ventured outside the desert compound. He lived in an old chicken coop beside the main adobe and took all of his meals alone. His life was his garden; he was masterful with things that grew.

Sometimes, when I went to town, I would return with a small gift for him. Once, I brought him a jar of cold, sweet grape juice. In the mid-day heat, he took the jar, gulped it down in six swallows, and as the juice dribbled down his chin, stared at me with what looked to be astonishment in his dark eyes. Another time I brought him a bundle of rawhide strips from a cobbler in Tucson.

In return, Hoosie brought me things: a snake's skull, a raven's feather, a ripe melon. He stood close to me and handled each object awkwardly, speaking softly and shyly in his own language, and when he thought it was the right time, he pushed the gift toward me, then turned and made his way back to his gardening.

Arizona, USA

In the evening, after Hoosie retired to his chicken coop for the night, Laura and I ate outside by candlelight at an old wooden table beside her flower garden. I escorted her to the table where salad, guacamole, bread, and chilled wine (which I had bought in Topowa) awaited us. We reached across the table and took each other's hands for the blessing.

Dining together in the evening became a ritual we looked forward to. We engaged in animated conversation in English, while she threw beguiling looks at me. Was she flirting? Was I flirting as I looked directly into her soft eyes and told her once again how special I thought she was?

But on the eighth evening, the day before I was scheduled to leave, something went horribly wrong. Laura became cold and distant. Instead of taking my hands in our ritual of grace, she scowled at me. There was pain and hurt and mistrust written all over her face. Had she fallen in love with a hippie traveler half her age only to realize it would inevitably lead to a dead end? What had I done, consciously or unconsciously, to bring us to this point?

Must I learn to be more ambiguous, appear to be inaccessible, disguise my innocent affection?

Chuck Choin. Born and bred in the "Divide Country." Colorado

The Sundown Family. "Gonna mosey up to the Gila Wilderness and live out our days there."
Arizona

Arizona, USA

Old Deschini was a Navajo healer, the first shaman I ever met. He was tall, silent, and mystical. He had luminous turquoise eyes, and his fingers were long, slender and rough like snakes.

To be with Old Deschini was, for me, to be transported back among pre-Columbian animists. I loved the way his moccasins barely touched the earth, the way his eyes pierced the desert brush to spy a sparrow's scratching, the way he gasped for oxygen as he inched along a steep canyon trail using finger holds no bigger than buttons.

Old Deschini cured Navajo neighbors of tuberculosis with wailing incantations that reminded me of Led Zeppelin, but his power extended far beyond such ceremonies. It was equally present, say, at a truck stop in Chinle, where he and I crawled under my van to inspect worn ball joints. Even there, his leathery face inched close to mine, his piercing blue eyes and clothing that smelled of sheep and dust, seemed not of this time and place but from long, long ago.

The last time I saw Old Deschini, he took me down into Canyon de Chelly. At his prompting I removed all my clothes and put them in a pile at the base of a juniper tree. The old man walked around in a circle for a minute or two — like an old brown lizard about to burrow in the sand — then pointed to a spot where he instructed me to lie down. Intoning in Navajo, he covered me up with hot sand, leaving only my head exposed. As he chanted, I understood the word "arthritis." Then, just like that, he left me, walking down the canyon and out of sight, never to be seen again.

Colorado, USA

I had always wanted to do a peyote ceremony with Native Americans. In the summer of 1976, circumstances led to its happening. On the Southern Ute Indian Reservation in Ignacio, two teenage boys had died falling out of a pickup. A peyote ceremony was organized to send their souls to Heaven.

I obtained permission to attend from the Chief but was blocked by the medicine man when I arrived at the site of the ceremony. He told me to stay away despite the chief's sanction. I paid him no heed and insisted, most disrespectfully, "I'm coming."

By midnight the wailing songs and prayers of the Indians and the intense hallucinations from the peyote juice had left me spent and scared. I went out to pee and lay down in the cool grass. The stars were comforting overhead. I didn't want to go back inside.

Things then happened so fast and violently that the stars and soft summer night vanished in a gasp. In their place I felt the sharp toe of a cowboy boot kicking me in the ribs and the medicine man's voice snarling, "Get your skinny white ass back into the ceremony, jerk. Don't you get it? Two boys are dead, their family devastated. You wanted this, now get back inside and do your part."

Eight hours later I crawled out of the sweat lodge feeling as though I had perished in a battle. The hallucinogenic glow had worn off and I left the reservation convinced I had trespassed and meddled where I had no business.

Utah, USA

I had some serious doubts as I mounted the rickety steps to "Sog" Shafer's trailer in Moab. What to expect from a man living beside a busy highway in one of the shoddiest homes I had ever seen? Once inside and face to face with him, however, I immediately fell under his spell and was soon convinced that I was in the presence of an alien intelligence or, at the very least, an eccentric genius. I sat in rapt attention as he proceeded to astound me with his historic and scientific knowledge. Turns out "Old Sog" had been everything from irrigation specialist, Colorado River navigator, and uranium miner to geologist, mathematician, explorer, and orchardist. "Christ, I could dowse with a witch hazel switch, find a trickle of water, follow it to an underground river, tap it, and make a whole forest of peach trees jump out of the desert."

After I left, I got to thinking that maybe the old fart was just the greatest bullshit artist on the planet — til I learned later from a third party about these amazing peaches plucked from an unexpected orchard on the edge of a Great Basin Desert.

Colorado, USA

After a three-week stay in my girlfriend's chic ski resort town of Telluride, I had had enough of the super rich and super cool, enough of hedonists in faux-frayed clothing, enough of Patagonia and Ralph Lauren. I took solace in wetback chambermaids, garbage men, dishwashers, janitors — anyone who wasn't absorbed in being "bitchin," "cool," "hip."

I was suffocating and wanted to scream from one end of the valley to the other. I prayed, "Lordy, Lordy, bring me someone authentic." And poof, it happened! An old cowboy, who might as well have just stepped off a dusty stage coach, got out of his battered '67 Dodge pickup while I was leaving the post office. I rubber-necked 180 degrees as he breezed into the building and instantly "knew" that he was "genuine."

Eagerly I introduced myself. His name was John Hawkes and, as I suspected, there was no hype, no pretense in him. He invited me to dinner, and I trailed him forty miles back to his ranch, like a heroine freak after a fix. My breathing, my pulse, were returning to "normal."

My evening with John and his wife, Trilby, eating together by kerosene lamp in the old parlor of their farmhouse, was like a scene out of a Zane Grey novel. Here was honesty and simplicity at last. For "dessert" John and his shepherd dog, Monty, howled duets together from the floor of my VW bus.

"Adios, Telluride."

New Mexico, USA

Her name was Luisa Lucero. She was a prairie midwife and herb gatherer in Roy. For almost fifty years — through snowstorms, dust bowls, depressions, and world wars — she had practiced her trade, traveling alone by horseback and wagon to the ranches and homesteads spread across the high New Mexican plains.

I visited Luisa on two occasions to gather her stories along with her medicinal herbs. We walked comfortably with one another, stooping to inspect a plant, gazing skyward to watch an eagle circle in the sky.

On each of our walks Luisa wandered away to sit alone on a hillock. There she would let the wind blow full in her face and her long white hair would curl in wisps about her head. At such times, she told me, she was remembering when she had been a practicing midwife on these prairies.

One night her cabin door had swung open and there stood a dark-skinned boy with worried eyes, breathing hard. He told her it was time to come help with a birthing. Telling her husband not to worry, she dressed hurriedly, followed the boy to his horse, mounted her own, and rode off to a distant light in the mountains where an anxious rancher's family listened for the sound of the horses. Louisa had delivered three hundred babies on these plains, three hundred rides deep into the hills.

Oregon, USA

In the mountain highlands of Umpqua National Forest, families emerge from rain-soaked tents to relax in the warming rays of morning sunshine. Six thousand people from all over America have gathered in a high alpine meadow to join in a week-long celebration of "love and understanding." It is called "The Rainbow Family Gathering," an event that takes place each year free and open to the public.

The highlight for me was the evening meal, communal food cooked in huge steaming caldrons in a forest clearing below giant Douglas firs. Thousands of hungry folks, chatting amicably, waited in the Great Meadow with their bowls and plates. A great silence followed, then a handful of participants began a magnificent chant of "Om." For fifteen minutes forest and sky filled with this mighty primordial noise — the sound of creation itself. Then … silence once again as our bowls were filled.

The scene was Biblical, a Cecil B. Demille epic of lost tribes coming to the desert to share an identity. Peace and fellowship propelled into the wild blue yonder by thousands of hearts pumping as one.

Arizona, USA

As a young traveler I spent a lot of time with my Navajo friend, Mary Tayah. Mary became my adoptive mother. She treated me like her own little boy and called me "Bahozoni," which meant "Everything Good In Front of You."

On the morning I was to leave — to drive a thousand miles into Mexico — Mary confessed that she had cancer. She looked like a scared sparrow standing beside her tin stove, her eyes downcast. She told me matter-of-factly that she was going to a doctor over in Tuba City, a distance of 160 miles, and that she had no option but to hitchhike alone, with no money, across the wind-blasted Colorado Plateau.

I cannot recall what I said or felt back then, standing next to her. What I do know is that I didn't offer to drive her to Tuba City, or to pay for the doctor. I know that, instead, I got in my camper and left. I can't remember how I said goodbye to her. Relatives wrote me a few months later that she had died.

Over the years, my failure to help Mary has haunted me. I used to make the excuse that I had been brought up wounded and desensitized in a fractured family that showed little evidence of caring or loving kindness. Now I'm inclined to think there are no excuses and take small comfort in the conviction that, next time, I would drive Mary to the ends of the Earth.

Oklahoma, USA

I am standing beside an old pump on an abandoned farm in the Panhandle. I let my hand touch the rusty handle. My mind wanders back through time to just before the great dust bowl storms, when there was still hope vested in the furrowed fields of soy beans and cotton. I look and listen — hear the father pumping life-giving water from the ground, see him proudly returning from town with a new bonnet for his wife. And there, behind the barn, they're serving guests homemade ice cream on their daughter's wedding day. How many generations lived here, barely making a "go" of it?

All gone now.

I grasp the pump handle,
    crank it twice, and feel in my bones
        the mournful song
it now sings.

North Dakota, USA

North Dakota is an ocean of light and silence. The solitary buzzing of a fly, the sound of a raven's wings, can stop you in your tracks.

Prairie sweethearts Don Elsbernd and Jacquie Restvedt stroll at sunset on the John Tissey Farm. Don, one of seven children, was raised on a nearby wheat farm, while Jacquie came here in 1976 to live where her father and grandfather and great grandfather had lived.

Don lost his right arm in a grain auger accident at age three.

Canada

I booked a flight on Calm Airways to Whale Cove, Nunavat, two hours north of Churchill on Hudson Bay. Whale Cove had been recommended to me by a Catholic priest who had spent forty years collecting Innuit artifacts for the mission museum there. While waiting in Churchill's airport, I lay up against my backpack on the floor and watched a group of Innuits who were also waiting for the flight. It was my first chance to look at the people I hoped to visit. They were a jolly bunch: toothless grandmothers laughing, young mothers nursing fat smiling babies, fishermen and hunters in rubber boots and T-shirts smoking cigarettes, and young boys and girls playing cat's cradle on the floor. Their eyes were dark and almond-shaped and they had soft round faces. All of them were speaking their native tongue, a mishmash of resonant clicks and grunts. Their hands and arms flew about with explosive exclamations. They were not the least self-conscious and lay on the floor as if they were in their living rooms. They called out to me and asked where I was going. When I told them Whale Cove, one fat old hunter did a funny pantomime, shivering with his arms about his waist, as if to say, "Ole Whitey gonna freeze his ass off," and everyone laughed.

Mexico

In San Miguel de Allende, Mexico, an old couple shuffles along a path on their way to a hovel beside a landfill to bed down on a stained mattress with exposed springs. Their names are Zoamillia and Martin Silva and they are at the end of their lives.

Nearly blind, incontinent, riddled with aches and pains — without money, home, friends, or family — they still have each other.

Estevan Urvina Perez was a 70-year-old campesino who eked out a living by selling brooms, wicker place mats and fans to fat cat clients at chic outdoor cafés in Patzcuaro. Local teenagers called him "Piggy" because he smelled so badly, a condition worsened by the boys peeing on him in the back alleys where he slept at night.

He told me that he chose to remain "smelly" so that the rich restaurant customers would be doubly irritated as he milled about their tables hoping for a sale. "My odor makes them so angry they buy something just to make me leave."

St. Vincent and the Grenadines

A mountain,

a hut,

a tethered cow.

If there was anything more,

my mind would explode.

St. Vincent and the Grenadines

On Union Island, one of the nine Grenadines, I met a man sitting on a box beneath a tree. In searing noon heat, he was hammering big stones into chips for the town's roadbed. Mopping his sweating face with a soiled cloth, he responded politely when I asked him how he liked this work. "I like it fine, sir. It be good work." He beamed and pointed, "Come tonight, I be livin' up dere, close to dem tamarind trees."

I arrived at dusk when the heat had abated and brought a cold beer for Mr. Ryan. "Oh, I's thankful t'you, sir, but I be afraid of strong drink. Come sit now." There were just two chairs, a small table, and a bed in his tiny cabin. Not even a mirror graced the bare walls. "Why, you don't even have a mirror, Mr. Ryan," I commented. "I never did court no vanity," he replied with eyes lowered modestly.

Here was a man who lived ever so simply, immune, it seemed, to material temptations, a man of Spartan economy and, as I learned from two hours of conversation, a man of utter devotion to Christ and the Gospel. Mr. Ryan, it turned out, was the island's preacher and its baptizer.

"In de old days, hear me now, de grandfadder was baptizer here 'bouts. He do things de island way, from slave times, y'know. When I was growed up, I took over da baptizing. Try to fill his shoes in dem ole ways. When a young'un — say ten year ole — come for baptizin', I lock 'em in de hut for a week wid only de water and de crackers. Oh Lordy, dey'd be on dere hands and knees waitin' for me. Dat way, I knows dey's was ready to receive de Lord!"

Boarding his sailboat on tiny Union Island, the captain took my hands and pulled me onto the deck. During the hour-long passage to neighboring Cariacou Island, I hunkered down in the open hold of the boat with a group of local islanders. We rested against large sacks of rice and corn and coconuts. The waves were running high from near gale–force winds and we were drenched from the spray. The captain stared straight ahead, his hand firmly on the tiller.

We were aboard a sailing cargo boat nearly 30 feet long. It had a mainsail and a jib, tacked well, and had good speed for being so heavy. I was told that this type of vessel, seldom seen these days, had been the freighter of choice in the Caribbean for the past 200 years.

Captain Festus Hutchinson was exceptionally tall and muscular. His head was finely shaped and his blue-green eyes were light and delicate. He had huge hands and feet and went without shoes. His poise would have inspired trust even in a hurricane.

Flautista, Caribe Indian. Commonwealth of Dominica

Ginger. "Let me sing you a song about the sea, women, babies, God, your soul." Commonwealth of Dominica

Shika was six when I met her in Ebenezer on the island of Antigua. She was one of nine grandchildren being raised by their grandmother, Mistress Susan Henry, a tall silent woman who worked tirelessly from dawn to dusk to provide food and clothing and moral direction for her brood.

Shika radiated innocence. She possessed no ill will, no guile whatsoever. She was as taintless and pure as new-fallen snow.

Whenever I invited the grandchildren to join my son, Taylor, and me at the beach, Shika always took my hand as we crossed the sere brown plains. Halfway there, we'd stop and rest in the shade of a cashie tree. Shika would crawl up on my lap. She smelled as sweet as lilac powder, and her smooth cheek upon my cheek was like a soft breeze from the hills. Her little voice was almost inaudible as she whispered to me about the distant sound of the surf or about the kid goat she had just seen jump off a rock. She was alive in herself and I felt her spriteliness, as if she was a tiny bejeweled bird or a fairy Tinkerbell!

Tarahumara girl. Herding sheep in a hail storm. Mexico

Dajabon girl. "We just got a water spigot in our house – first time ever!"
The Dominican Republic

Antigua and Barbuda

I was hiking in the hills above Ebenezer going no place in particular, prepared to meet whomever, when I came across a man with a grey donkey. The man was sitting on the ground eating a tamarind fruit. I heard him say something that I couldn't quite understand and drew near to him. He repeated the words in a low gravelly voice. I tilted my head and cocked an ear, as if my hearing had deceived me. Once again, the man rasped out his greeting.

"Life is good," is what I thought he said.

"What did you say?" I asked.

"Life is good," the man repeated and his face burst into a huge smile.

His name was David Lincoln. He lived below in town. He was up in the bush looking for his goats.

He chortled some, remained sitting, chewing on the tamarind. I sat down next to him but our conversation, which I kept trying to steer toward the weather or his goats or his life, never seemed to click.

"Life is good."

What more, after all, needed to be said?

Costa Rica

Lambert "Buzo" Williams, 62, is the "scorned one" in flashy Cahuita. He is at the bottom of the heap, the one who can't afford a proper shack, or shoes, or even a shirt to keep the scorching sun off his back. He lives in a filthy tent that lacks a fly and screen door, inviting both rain and biting insects. He cobbles meals from dumpsters and cooks them over dry coconut husks in a hubcap. He lies around in the park with other "dead-beats" who, in the shadows of dusk, resemble mangy, flea-bitten curs.

Buzo has lived in Cahuita all his life. "Me worked hard on farm, took care of goats and horses and mules. Worked wid de machete all my life in de bush. Snakes, scorpions, jaguars, dem things don't scare me. If I be starvin', I eat pickled monkey livers like how dem old ones get by in de slave days."

I treat Buzo to dinners out. He is partial to "rondon" (fish in spicy coconut milk) and has no qualms disdaining utensils and dining without his shirt while seated next to tourists in the scented candlelight of fancy eateries. He always hands me a bag of fruit he has scavenged in the jungle as repayment. "I don't be beholdin' to nobody."

Half the cafés and restaurants in Cahuita have "No Buzo edicts," especially the famous "Coco's," an upscale Italian lounge. He and I once tried for a table, only to be evicted by the owner. "Hell, mon, dis land where Coco's at belong once to my family," he carped as we were ushered out. "There'll come a day when de tables are turned and them Coco bastards will come crawlin' to old Buzo to beg fruit and fish and snake meat. I know how to forage good, mon. I can survive. You wait 'til de oil runs out and all dem tourists don't come no more, and we'll see who go hungry round here. Not Buzo, dat for sure."

Nicaragua

Ricardo Hernandez made twelve cents an hour picking coffee beans on slippery mountain trails. Each of his bags weighed one hundred pounds and had to be hauled by hand half a mile downslope to a collection point. It was the only job he could get to provide for a wife and four kids. I chose him from a line of fifty starving men and women awaiting their pay at the end of the day.

Everything about him spoke of a man pushed to the limits by poverty and the grind of daily life. His clothing was stained with sweat and dirt, his leather sandals were ripped. His eyelids sagged, his lips trembled, and his shoulders slouched.

His face was a kaleidoscope of emotions. He might as well have been born to misery in Turkey or Bolivia or India. He was "everyman" who has never known rest or security or hope.

Jamaica

The first time I saw "Che," he was barefoot and naked, save for his boxers. He was moving very fast across a field, wild-eyed like Ben Gunn, and seemed to be seeking a hiding place from captors in hot pursuit. At his waist he wore a "cutlass" and in his hand he brandished a smoldering stick which he kept blowing on. "Where are you going?" I shouted as he sped past me, jumping from stone to stone like Gollum. "I's bound for me goats, mon, high up in da bush at 'Percy's.' I's starving! Need goat meat, mon." He invited me to join him.

I accompanied him to "Percy's," running as we went. He led me high up the mountain to a long-lost jungle where he grew yams and stashed them in gunnysacks. "Dis be where da slaves hid out an' dem Caribes an' Arawaks too." Che made a fire from dry coconut husks, the smoke forming a halo about his head. "Dis is where I be safe. No one to bodder wid you here. No neighbor folk, no one telling you put on shirt, pants. I lives like dem Maroons from rebel times. Dat's what I likes to be, one of dem Maroons. But got daughters an' grandkids down in de town I needs to hep feed."

Back at his austere house of concrete blocks, Che cooked up gristly strips of goat meat skewered on green sticks. His two rooms were bare except for a tick mattress and a primitive earthen stove. When the meat was done, he ripped at it with his teeth. I followed suit. "Goat meat good, mon. Make you strong like Maroon soldier, strong so you'se can cut de throats of three of dem slave captors — three at once!"

Pauline and Mr. Christian. "We share dominoes on a slow day."
Antigua and Barbuda

Ladakhi father and son. "The land of the broken moon." India

Sister Ina Campbell. "Let me be small so I can be with God." Jamaica

Eva Soto. "By the grace of God I will go to the 'little angel' field tomorrow to work our corn." Bolivia

Haiti

I lived with a Haitian family in a small agricultural town called Gros Jean, a half hour bus ride from the capital. It was common here to see a woman hiking a mile down a mountain and returning with a pail of water on her head and one in each hand. I traveled on foot with my cameras some five miles a day asking people if they would oblige me a portrait. Most said no. I tried to sweeten the deal by offering a few dollars, but they could not be persuaded. Were they ashamed of their poverty? Were they suspicious of any outsider after centuries of oppression by despots both foreign and domestic? Was there a voodoo-related taboo associated with cameras and the soul-stealing power of photos? Or was it just defiant pride? They didn't want anyone "possessing" one of the last things they could call their own, images of themselves.

The grandmother pictured here assented. Perhaps the click of a camera in return for two dollars allowed her to stay home that day and rest. Maybe she desperately needed cash for medicines to keep a sick grandchild alive. Or maybe — who knows — she might have just said to herself, "Bon Dieu, if he wants a picture of a proud and courageous woman, then I be that!"

Haiti

One day I went to a fair in the mountains near Forêt des Pines. Three thousand country folk had come on foot or donkey to sell home-cooked meals and garden produce. I wormed my way in, the only white person present, and immediately began shooting film.

I was drunk on the scene and ploughed through the crowd for three hours, like a machine gunner mowing down everything in front of him. I didn't ask anyone for permission, and if they scowled at me, which the woman in the foreground is doing, I shot anyway. I didn't cough up a single dime to help these people, by buying, say, a meal or a pumpkin.

Fifteen years later this image haunts and shames me. I have yet to speak of it when I give photography classes at high schools. Haitians, I am sorry!

Guatemala

In 1981 I lived in an Indian village in the rain forest. During my first week in San José Petén, I bought an old thatch-roofed cottage on Lake Petén's shore. It was a typical Mayan house, its interior mud-walled with skinned upright poles and rafters lashed together with vines. The roof leaked, the walls were caving in, and at night I could hear rats scurrying about in the thatch while giant cockroaches scampered across the floor like miniature race horses. It was not a house my father, who was raised in the lap of Connecticut luxury, would have been caught dead in, but I liked its earthy simplicity.

From my kitchen window I could look out upon the lake and watch the villagers paddling their dugouts to market. In the evening I sat on my doorstep and watched the men returning from their small garden plots in the jungle, machetes at their sides. Barefoot boys dressed in white and beaming with pride led donkeys laden with heavy sacks of corn and beans past my hut. Saddles creaked amid the strong smell of lather and sweat and dust. This "parade" had been occurring here nightly for hundreds of years.

Guatemala

My two favorite children in the village were little sisters, Loyda and Beti. They were the children of Alicia and Isaro, my neighbors next door. Because their hut was so close to mine — eleven feet to be exact — the girls were in my house every minute of every day, warbling like songbirds.

When suppertime came, I would shoo all the neighborhood children home to their parents, but I always made an exception for Loyda and Beti. We then had the whole house to ourselves. Beti would go down to the lake to fetch fresh water, while Loyda did the dishes on the hearth. A softness would descend on the cottage while the wind rustled the palms overhead and the waves lapped gently on the beach.

We snuggled together on the bed, strung beads, and told jokes. Sometimes I read to them, other times told them stories that I made up as I went along. Then Alicia's voice would break the reverie: "Beti! Loyda! Venga! Tiempo para dormir." And they would jump up, kiss me goodnight, and skip out the door like fireflies.

Guatemala

I was reminded of humanity's dark side when I lived those two winters in Guatemala. The early 80's were years of great repression and terror throughout the country. I would lie awake at night in my hut by Lake Petén Itza and tremble, fearing the worst at my door. Would it be rebels or government troops who would crash through and abduct me?

I learned quickly that no one in my village could be trusted, therefore one never spoke of politics. Never! Brothers were known to turn on brothers, sisters on sisters, children might denounce their own parents.

This portrait I made of thirteen-year old Costura reminds me of Jesus. The wire crossing Costura's head could be a substitute for thorns, an emblem of innocence, which is an invitation for persecution by those in power. Costura was young, female, and a pureblooded Mayan, threefold liabilities in what was then a fragmented and paranoid country.

Ladakhi mountain woman. "Winter is the time for Buddhist practices."
India

Mistress Cluden, midwife. "Oh Lordy, I think I've birthed everybody!"
Union Island, St. Vincent and the Grenedines

England

During my stay in the Yorkshire Dales I especially liked visiting with Willie Bentham, either at the Sun Pub where we played dominoes or at his small house in Dent where he would cook mutton on an open fire. "Will ye take a bit o' meat, lad?" he would always ask me before he launched into the next installment of the "Blizzard of 1948."

I was staying across the Dale at Shoolbred Farm, on a hillside in Flo and Joe Hartley's hay barn. Joe, who grew up with Willie, was always asking me to invite his old buddy for tea. Flo would snicker, "Aye, Willie will ne're come. He's just too odd an old bachelor to be regular-like and social."

I asked Willie time and again to come for tea with his old friends. "Nay, nay, I shant't intrude on Joe and Flo. Tisn't me style." Finally one day when I had beseeched him yet again, he surprised me by saying, "Aye."

Willie arrived promptly at five o'clock, took off his rain gear, and fell into Yorkshire idiom with Joe about sheep and the "clashy" weather. Flo put the finishing touches on the meal she was cooking on her wood stove. "Come to the table, lads, time to eat." Willie dragged himself to the table without getting out of his chair.

In the middle of the meal, Willie rummaged in his baggy trousers, brought out a jar of pickled onions and placed them on the table. Perhaps a present for his old friends, I thought. Willie unscrewed the lid and dished a dozen onions onto his plate — between the duck eggs and bacon — then screwed on the lid and returned the jar to his trousers pocket. "I'll take a little more tea, Flo," he said as if nothing had happened. Flo kicked me under the table and gave me a wink. Joe raised his eyebrows and chortled.

England

John Bentham, 19, was destined to be a bachelor, as was his younger brother, Thomas. Their parents would see to it — no wifely distractions to get in the way of keeping up East Banks, their old farm in the Yorkshire Dales. The lads didn't seem bothered by the prospect. Said John, "I was born and bred to be a farmer. I want nothing more."

The brothers knew every cranny of the local dale, from Dent Head to Dent Foot, from Whernside Mountain to Comb Scar, and everything in between. While afoot with a pack of border collies or from a Land Rover, they mustered their livestock with mechanical precision.

On occasion, I would help the lads herd sheep or mark "tups" (young rams) or drive their Limousin and Charolais cattle to drink at "Bottoms." At night, after the tea dishes had been washed and put away and the parents had retired, John would get down his Book of Breeds and quiz his young brother. "Tell me, Thomas, what distinguishes a Corriedale from a Swaledale? Why would Welsh mountain sheep fare poorly in the Dales? What's a 'mule gimmer'?"

The farm had no TV, no video games, no Internet. Rather, the Benthams' interest lay elsewhere, in cultivating the ancient bloodlines of their sheep, cattle, ponies, even dogs, the old-fashioned way, without the aid of computers or other electronic wizardry. Some of that old blood surely coursed through the veins of John and Thomas as well.

Because many of the South Uist islanders only spoke Gaelic, I often traveled with a young boy by the name of Ian Paul MacInnes who spoke both Gaelic and English. We liked tramping on the remote eastern shore of the island, across the trackless moors and over the barren hills. Ian told me how he respected the people "of the east" for they were great walkers, strong workers, and hearty individualists. Roads, electricity, and telephones had only arrived here in the 1970s.

I loved Ian Paul as a father loves a son. I got to know him the winter of 1981 when I was collecting stories of the islanders and living in the MacCormick's hayloft. My favorite image of Ian Paul is of him at the feet of the old sea captain, John MacKillob, who is serving us tea and whiskey and holding us rapt with whaling tales.

Ian Paul was killed at twenty-seven in a tragic hunting accident. He and his older brother had gone off to shoot geese on a nearby moor. A shot was fired that hit Ian Paul and he died shortly afterward.

He will forever remain in my mind my twelve-year-old "son."

Scotland

I often went looking for the old herdsman, asking crofters at the edge of the machair if they had seen him. Once I found him sitting in an old cellar hole in his oilskins, ruminating in the pouring rain. "John," I said, "how long have those stepping stones been there to help travelers across the marsh?" "Oh," he droned, "they'd be older than the village and older still than the castle. T'was the Vikings put them there a long time ago."

I never visited Donald John MacClellan without bringing him food and drink: oat cakes and cheese, a carrot for his horse, a scrap of meat for his dog, and always the wee dram of whiskey. Sometimes we drank in silence, the howling wind and driving rain smothering our voices. He told me that at times like these he would prefer to have one drink upon the moor than twenty in a warm hotel.

I was in awe of Donald John's solitary life as a shepherd. From first light until dusk, year after year, he wandered the barren moors with his herds of sheep and cattle. His life was bound up with things simple and elemental: wind and rain, sunlight and snow, the warmth of a peat fire; a marsh bird announcing the coming of spring, its speckled eggs discovered at the nest; dappled light on frozen marsh grass; the world reflected in a sheep's eye.

Willie MacPherson and Peter Haggerty. "Willie, look west and behold St. Kilda." Scotland

"Bee" MacPhee and Ian. "Aye, we keep the cattle for the boy, teaches him attention and responsibility." Scotland

Scotland

It was a glorious autumn evening on South Uist in the Outer Hebrides. Rays of light in the rain-soaked sky made everything bright and shining. The shore grasses shimmered in luminous greens, the beaches were pure white, and our skin glowed with a rich orange, the color of peaches. We were playing "hide and seek."

The children took turns leading me to their favorite hiding places. Reflecting basic gender differences, the boys liked the high knolls of rock crags where the woolly sheep slept while the girls preferred the gentleness of the tall, soft grasses that lay between the tide pools and marshes.

"Ninety-eight, ninety-nine, one hundred. Ready or not, here I come." Dolina and I lay next to each other, flat on our backs, breathing hard, our hearts racing. We waited, listened, and heard Angus John's footsteps on the ground nearby. Our breathing became slower, rhythmic, in unison. Sea birds circled overhead and shouts of Gaelic rose in the air. Marsh grasses bent and swayed above us, and the world seemed round and full, spinning for long minutes without weight or form. Then Angus John crashed through the tall grass and looked down at us like some triumphant crofter about to squash a nest of weevils. We made a pathetic attempt to run for the goal to save ourselves, but Angus John was like a gazelle, beating us by a hundred strides.

Scotland

In a remote corner of Scotland's Outer Hebrides, Kate Effie MacCormick lived a traditional life with her sister and two brothers. She and I developed a game which we played daily. Each morning I would rise from my sleeping bag in the hay barn and walk to the house for breakfast. Kate Effie would be waiting at the door, a frying pan in her hand and the same question for me: "Have you brought the ring from America? If not, there shan't be any porridge and eggs for you, laddie." I would play my part and dig deep in both pockets to search for the ring but only pull out strands of hay. Then Kate Effie would pull my ear and swear at me in Gaelic. She called me "hockenoch" (numb skull) which made her brothers laugh. This charade went on for the four months I stayed with the MacCormicks, though I often wondered if she truly wished to go to America with a barn-dwelling waif!

Once, while she was standing in a biting wind washing clothes by hand in cold water, I approached her from behind and waited. When she felt my presence, she turned slowly, clutching a pair of bib overalls with swollen red hands and gazed at me with all her womanliness. There was a calm radiance in her eyes that bespoke self-assurance and wisdom. A look that would last an eternity.

Had her parents permitted her to marry as a young woman, Kate Effie would have made a sturdy homesteader and partner. Her heart was pure. She cared for her three siblings until they died, and then, as neighbors later wrote, went very quickly to her own death.

Scotland

While tramping around the island of South Uist one day, I came upon a stone cottage close to the sea. Behind it was an extraordinary curiosity, a bus covered in shells.

Of course, I went right up to the cottage and knocked. A white-haired woman in glasses and wearing a house smock peered out at me. "Have ye come for the tour?" she asked in a thick brogue. "I guess I have," I responded.

She led me into the bus where a dizzying array of knick-knacks, all made from sea shells, cluttered every space. "It was just an eyesore lying vacant and derelict out back of our cottage, and, well, when me dear husband passed on, I got the notion to spruce it up. I made hundreds of trips to the shore to fill me baskets with shells. I glued thousands of them to the outside, then made me way to the inside. Took me only three months."

"I get twenty-five cents for the guided tour. People come here from all over to behold what can be made beautiful from ordinary things. With the proceeds, I make a yearly donation to the Multiple Sclerosis Foundation of Scotland. MS, y'see, is the disease that took me dear husband."

Wales

Nearing the end of his life, the old carpenter had little to do now on the estate. Where once his great strength had been used to lift a wagon to repair a wheel or to hoist boulders for a wall, he was now relegated to repairing chairs or polishing the andirons for the "Big House." Hughie "Hen Gae" Jones still worked a five-day week, but time weighed heavily on him in the carriage house where he waited anxiously for the estate owner to assign him a task.

I visited him regularly on my bicycle during my months in Llanfachreth town. He seemed to perk up when I arrived and would launch into yet another history lesson about Wales, the Estate, the village. When I asked him if he had served with the Allies in World War II, Hughie's eyes came to life.

As he described his war exploits beside a roaring fire, his arms would fly out to the side, his mouth would spit with emphasis, and finally, unable to control himself, he would revert to Welsh! In his retelling of those horrific years, I transformed him into a fierce Celtic warrior battling Roman invaders with scythes and clubs and their own fists. How paltry mending a chair or polishing andirons must seem compared to his war deeds.

Ireland

Of the three Aran Islands, I chose tiny Inisheer to visit. It was described by fellow travelers as a starkly beautiful place, webbed by loose stone walls separating small fields. Although visited regularly by ferries out of Galway, the island was said to have preserved much of its dignity and unspoiled character. As I disembarked with hundreds of other tourists clamoring to experience the "real Ireland," a feeling of being just another voyeur swept over me.

Determined not to be one of them, I quickly outdistanced the gawking crowds and emerged alone in a remote corner of the island. I soon came upon a man gathering potatoes in his "lazy beds." We stared at each other without cordialities for nearly a minute, as if I were the hunter who had located my prey and was contemplating the manner with which to dispatch it.

"No doubt, you've come like the rest of the mob to see us. Well, here I am," he said quietly. "Please take my picture, for that's what you want, isn't it? I have no objection."

I took out my camera and snapped the shutter, a single picture of an Inisheer man. As I thanked him and asked his name, I felt that I had somehow violated him and desecrated the scene. "Colin McPhee," he said. I gleaned nothing more from him though in truth I yearned to sit with him over tea or beer, have a smoke together. I had deluded myself into thinking that I was a traveler and not a tourist, that I was sensitive and caring, a head above the rest. I should have known better.

Travel, Ethan, is not a *carte blanche* affair. It is, rather, a potentially corrupting, irreversible, intrusive influence you must guard against at all costs.

Portugal

This old Portuguese couple from Moimenta surprised me on the trail, appearing as if from nowhere. They stood motionless, like statues, radiating calm and warmth.

They were carrying chestnuts and, from what little Portuguese I understood, I gathered that they had spent all day, every day, for a month, collecting the nuts for storage in the valley below. They had already harvested fourteen gunnysacks full! Knowing how long it had taken me to fill up one sack, I was as staggered by their fortitude as by their gentle grace, their soft, stress-free expressions.

Imagine! Composure bred of a lifetime of hard hand labor. I wonder if their faces would be less content and accepting had their world not been unhurried, unmechanized, uncluttered — had they been field workers, say, in the modern impersonal pressure cooker of my culture.

Portugal

I am gathering chestnuts in Moimenta with two unmarried sisters and their unmarried brother, an old-fashioned threesome who drive a donkey cart everywhere. The sisters are Dometilde and Araminda and their brother is Alvaro (whom I witnessed clasping his hat to his heart in prayer last Sunday in church). I try to be of assistance in the harvest but the three of them outpace me easily.

For two evenings now, I have called upon them at their old home which once belonged to their parents. We four gather around a huge open fireplace where they cook their food. They insist that I share a meal of potatoes and meat with them. I tell them in bad Spanish and pantomime that my hostess, Maria, has already fed me (I stick out my stomach and my cheeks) but they will not be dissuaded by my theatrics.

I end up at their table where we suck on bones of mutton and eat roasted potatoes with our fingers. We toast with good red wine they have made in their barn. For dessert, Alvaro carefully digs out of the coals three small apples that have been baking while we eat. He takes pride in knowing when they are perfectly done and draws them out with a small rake. He then puffs up his red cheeks into miniature bellows and with his breath neatly blasts off the charred skin, leaving nothing but pure white pulp. Dometilde pours honey on them and beams.

France

At a three-month-long meditation retreat at Lerab Ling in the Massif Central, my teacher Sogyal Rinpoche introduced his students to "the Nature of Mind." The setting was a large shrine tent. Three hundred people from all over the world — I among them — sat on colorful cushions on the floor facing Rinpoche. He told us that at the count of three, he would snap his fingers and utter an indescribable "click" in the back of his throat. This would be the sign for us to begin our meditation.

I peeked at my watch and noted the position of the second hand. "Click!" I let go of my discursive mind and fell into an inner peace and silence. The entire tent seemed to pulse in reds and blacks, like infrared film, and there was a palpable "vibration" throughout the gathering. In all my years meditating, I had never achieved such a level of "no mind." I felt blissed out. Then Rinpoche snapped his fingers, and we all came back to earth. I noted that the elapsed time was forty-five seconds.

Rinpoche smiled, as usual, but warned that what had just taken place should not be discussed at dinner. "Keep any realizations to yourself," he counseled.

Of course, we couldn't resist sharing notes at dinner. The dining room was on fire with our buzzing. Everyone, it seemed, had had the same amazing experience.

When we had gathered the next morning, Rinpoche smiled at us and said, "So ... I hear you all compared notes about your meditation yesterday. You all found the experience to be extraordinary. You know what I think is extraordinary? That you refuse to go there on your own every moment of your lives.

Wake up now!"

Oliver. Banana picker. Commonwealth of Dominica

Quechua couple. "Ours is the last lived-in Inca town." Peru

Peru

The scenery from Cuzco to the Sacred Valley in Peru transitions from the coarse to the sensual. The city's confusion of noise and concrete, its littered outskirts, give way to groves of eucalyptus and sleepy villages of mud-and-wattle houses.

Somewhere before the ancient town of Pisac, the bus screeches to a halt in front of a cluster of shabby thatch-roofed adobes. The door opens and an Indian boards. He makes his way to an empty seat just behind the driver.

It is my first intimate encounter with a South American Indian. I try to soak up his essence, like litmus paper, straining to smell him, avidly listening to him suck on a wad of cocoa leaves balled up in his cheek. I can't help staring at his leathery, brown skin and his bright red hand-woven poncho, hat, and pants. Like a vermillion hummingbird he has alighted two seats in front of me. His attire might as well have been in neon flashing at me: "Yes, I am Indian. My ancestors looked just like this before Pizarro was even born!"

Peru

At dusk I hike up a stony trail toward alpine meadows that rise up like Mongolian steppes. I am bound for Huilloc village where I have made new friends. Huilloc is a traditional Quechua (Incan) village at close to 11,000 feet, one of the very last of its kind in Peru. Passing a rude mud house with smoke pouring through its blackened thatch roof, I meet four school children playing "blind man's bluff." I approach stealthily, signaling "silencio" with raised finger to my lips. The girl with the cloth around her eyes continues to grope for the others. I draw nearer and put myself in her path. Soon she finds me, reading me, as it were, with her fingers. We have to bite our lips to keep from laughing, we four "sighted" ones, that is. Soon her mouth explodes in laughter as she blurts out, "Eres tu, Luis, eres tu!" (I go by the name "Luis" in South America as "Ethan" doesn't seem to compute.) She removes her blindfold, sees that it is indeed me, and we five hold each other and jump up and down with childish joy.

Peru

In the wan light of dusk, I walk with two little boys beside a field of corn in Ollantaytambo. We walk hand in hand in silence toward the boys' grandfather who awaits their return. The old man, large boned and sturdy like the trunk of a massive tree, stands patiently watching as we approach, He wears a shabby hat and his clothes are frayed, but his bearing is proud and strong despite his years. He smiles and offers me his large, coarse hand as his eyes accept me. Here he is, standing at the edge of his corn field at the end of a long life of unimaginable toil. Yet his smile and kind demeanor seem to say, it's okay, Luis, just take it step by step down the road. I sigh and, giving the old man a strong hug around his broad shoulders, look down at the brown earth with its green shoots of corn. The four of us then walk quietly back to town.

Peru

I returned to Ollantaytambo, Peru, soon after my four-month stay there. My backpack contained two hundred images of Quechua people I had previously photographed. They were thrilled to receive the photos. Many of my subjects had never seen or owned a picture of themselves.

Wood gatherer. He smelled of smoke and sap and sweat. Peru

Juan Branco, shepard. Portugal

Greece

I lived for a month in a garret in an old house on Lesvos, a mountainous island in the northern Aegean Sea. The space belonged to an elderly widow named Heleni. In exchange for lodging, I hauled wood, carried water from the town well, and tended her small flock of goats.

Heleni was a tiny woman, barely five feet tall. She was badly stooped from old age and when she swept out her rooms, her head nearly touched her knees. She went about the day laughing and smiling and talking to herself.

The warm days of late fall quickly passed. Skim ice appeared on the cattle troughs around the town of Ayassos. My room in the garret grew frigid, and I could see my breath even in the middle of the day. When the snows came at the beginning of December, Heleni, her dog Muesel, and I began to spend much of our time around a small, rectangular sheet metal stove in her living room.

We were cozy by the stove and we lazed about like stoned teenagers. We ate sumptuous lamb stews and casseroles, cabbages and carrots in olive oil, all of it soaked up with fresh bread. We savored pastry and drank strong Greek coffee from small white porcelain cups filled to the rim.

We were happy together, spread out on the big yellow pillows with Muesel curled up with us. Heleni lacked for nothing in her simple life.

180

Sonoran rancher. "You want to see ancient cave paintings in the mountains?" Mexico

Papas Mikhalis. "I will always pray for you." Cyprus

Macedonia

In a small village near Bitola, I met Peta, 78, who had once been the greatest slalom skier in his country, selected to represent his nation in the Olympics. He now lived in a dilapidated house, bedridden much of the time with an arthritic hip. His chief concern was caring for his old horse, once the finest steed in town.

I made this portrait of Peta and his horse in front of a decaying "wedding carriage" that had, over a lifetime of 35 years, carried young brides to local churches. Peta had been the driver. Now the wheels of the carriage were half-buried in weeds, and the wooden sideboards had nearly disintegrated. The seat had crumpled into fragments, where once it had held blushing brides festooned with flowers. Peta, the horse, and the carriage appeared to be in equal stages of decay.

Cyprus

During the long days of spring, ancient brown-skinned men perch silently, like regal old birds, against the immaculate white walls of their mountain village, Treis Elies. They seem suspended in time — comfortable, innocuous, purposeless.

Nestoras, Christakis, and Andreas: enjoying the moment, nothing left to say. Ten thousand incidents, ten thousand stories — all sequestered deep within each of them now.

There they sit, brethren bonded by long lives shared, their pasts merged and forgotten in a moment of warm spring sunshine falling on their tired shoulders.

Kosovo

Arjeta Topojani (with students in photo) taught school in Kushnin village. To get there from home, she used to walk for two often harrowing hours, then repeat the ordeal at the end of the day. There were days in winter when she plodded in the dark through waist-deep snowdrifts, often accompanied by an icy wind. During spring snowmelt she had to row herself across a dangerously swollen river. On hot autumn days she kept an eye out for adders on the trail. Throughout the Serb occupation, soldiers routinely harassed her on her daily treks. During the two years of the war, Arjeta received no salary for her work.

"How did I do it, you ask. I believed that one day Kosovo would be independent of Serbia, free to pursue its own course, its schools liberated from prying Belgrade eyes. It was a dream so powerful, I gave myself to my country's cause with every ounce of my strength in the only capacity available to me, as a teacher."

Kosovo

Alone among the villagers in Kushnin, only Adem Shatri and his wife, Jyl, still transport goods in a wagon, pulled by a yoke of oxen. Everyone else in town has a car or pickup truck.

"When I was a boy, there were a hundred ox teams here to plow the fields and pull wagons. My father and I used to go into the mountains to fell big trees that we made into wagons and yokes. I am proud that my wife and I still get about in a wagon. I wouldn't ever want to own a car."

As Adem carried on, Jyl grabbed my arm, and speaking through an interpreter, pleaded, "Merciful Allah, why, oh why, doesn't Adem get rid of those stupid oxen and that useless cart that shakes my innards into jelly. Why do we still own something from the time of Alexander the Great. Why can't we be normal like everyone else. Adem, for Allah's sake, let's get a car!"

Egypt

I hitched a ride across the Sahara in Egypt with a man named Sharif and his two small sons, Omar and Mahmood, their eyes soft, their faces dusty. The battered old pickup truck was loaded down with crates of white chickens.

The "Chicken Express" left Bahoreya Oasis at sunset for our destination, Farafra Oasis. The desert sky was aflame in orange and red. Along the 200 km dirt track there were half a dozen army check posts at each of which Sharif bribed the grimy-faced guards with a present of a squawking chicken. On we went, mile after mile through a section called the White Desert, the road illuminated by a cold full moon. We ate sandwiches that I made while Sharif drove, his pita bread and my cheese and tuna fish, the four of us gobbling the crusty mess at 50 bumpy mph. My window was stuck open as was Sharif's, and the cold desert wind chilled us. I put on my "galibea" smock and wrapped Omar and Mahmood in a blanket, their precious warmth against my legs heaven sent.

I thought, here I am doing what I've always wanted to do … riding across the Sahara in moonlight. I looked at the faces of my three companions, desert Arabs, draped in scarves with their deep rich dark skin, the whites of their eyes shining. We got bogged down five times, had to dig ourselves out, but the "Chicken Express" arrived on time the next day at Farafra Oasis.

"Allah wa akbar," Praise God!

Egypt

My favorite time in Farafra Oasis occurred in the afternoon when animals and families were coming home from the fields, water girls carrying copper and clay pots on their heads, young boys in tunics leading white donkeys and their foals to water troughs. Dark cattle, flocks of woolly sheep, chickens being driven to roost — all creating clouds of dust that settled on the palm fronds.

192

Egypt

I spent much of my time at the oasis in Sharif's garden. I always entered it as I might enter a cathedral, coming in out of the heat with a need for sanctuary, silence, the cooling color of green, light filtered and dappled by a thousand palm fronds. In the garden's shade the temperature was at least ten degrees cooler, the ground a carpet of clover, balm to my hot and sweating feet.

Little Omar and his friend, Saben, would come in with me. While I read, they would clean my sun glasses or the blades of my Swiss Army knife. Sometimes they would snatch my camera and snap pictures of me in secret. Bird song, a cricket chirping from a hollow log, the muted voices of the nearby street, and the muezzin's scratchy voice from the far end of the oasis reaching me faintly, as if in a dream.

South Africa

I am on the East Cape beside the Indian Ocean living in the Kraal Hostel with a handful of world travelers from England, Israel, France, Italy, Canada, Ireland, and Mexico. We form a well-integrated family and are regaled by the Xhosa staff (Big Cynthia, Precious, Constance, and Fundiswa) as equals, as friends. Every night after dinner white travelers and black cooks party together to the music of James Brown and Bob Marley.

In stark contrast, when I visit nearby Coffee Bay to go to the bank, I find myself the only white man in a sea of Africans, immediately lose all my confidence, become utterly paranoid, and give gatherings of men the widest possible berth. As I walk through town, I feel excluded, resented, powerless. A pariah. Apartheid's legacy in reverse.

South Africa

Big Cynthia was head cook at the Kraal Hostel on East Cape and found favor with us "travelers" by making Wednesday and Saturday nights "pizza nights."

Last night, after we all helped the staff clean and organize the kitchen, Big Cynthia decided to sample some tequila sunrises that Lennie from Newton, Massachusetts, had concocted. Cynthia seemed to like them very much — so much so that by midnight she had stumbled down to the beach below the hostel and was floundering and vomiting in the pounding surf.

I went down to meet her with towels and warm soapy water and cleaned her up as best as I could, speaking softly to her and stroking her cold, trembling forehead. It was a chilly, damp night with intermittent sprinkles and a whipping wind. Telling her not to worry, I ran to the bunkhouse and brought back my sleeping bag and extra blankets, then held her in my arms for several hours.

Come breakfast, Big Cynthia was once again on hand to feed us, an embarrassed look on her face but still the big caring woman we loved.

I left for Cape Town that afternoon, hauling my duffle bag and tent to a dump truck. After saying goodbye to all the kitchen staff as well as my tribe of travelers, I threw my gear into the truck but had difficulty hoisting myself into its high back. In a flash I felt big strong arms lifting me skyward as if I were as light as a forty-pound sack of grain. It was Big Cynthia, my Xhosa friend, thanking me and saying goodbye in her own way.

Grandmother and baby on a quiet summer's day. Senegal

Grandmother and granddaughter. "One day Banta, you will become like me."
Senegal

India

Tsetan, a Tibetan horse trekking guide on a windy plain. At sixteen thousand feet there are no villages, only the wind, the cold, and occasional shepherds' huts — crude chambers with three-foot thick stone walls.

India

Late one afternoon in Ladakh, Tsetan and I got drunk on two large bottles of beer. We ran helter-skelter down the valley, hooting and hollering and carrying on, as the horses frolicked after us with their reins dragging on the ground. Tsetan surprised me by crossing the swollen river on one of the horses, laughing as he rode it backward through the rapids. He came back on foot, gathered me up in his strong arms, and carried me to the other side where we made a fire and fell asleep in a pile of leaves.

India

At Shing-O on the Tibetan plateau I came upon two young sisters who were harvesting root crops in a small garden by a stable. I watched them from afar, drawing close only when I felt they had accepted my presence. For the next several afternoons, as the sun arced above us, we pulled carrots and smooth-skinned potatoes from the cold ground. The black composted soil smelled of decay and yeast. Sometimes we inched so deliciously close that our fingers touched and our breath warmed each other's cheeks. Once I threw a smooth round stone into the collecting basket and pretended it was a potato. The sisters erupted in laughter and chastened me by slapping my hand.

India

In September Tsetan and I stayed with a family of shepherds from the lowlands of Ladakh. They were the last people in the highlands with their herds at this late season. The roof of their two-room hut was covered with stretched hides, carcasses of sheep and goats drying in the sun. Lean dogs were slinking about the grounds.

The family consisted of two old grandparents with smudged faces; a father with long hair and a woolly beard; a mother in skins who milked the yaks and chanted Buddhist scripture with deep moans; three strong brothers who rode fast horses across the dusty plains; and five beautiful daughters with long black hair and flashing smiles.

They fed us roast yak and turnips for supper. Afterwards I rested on a pile of sheepskins in the corner of the hut. Before retiring for the night, I brought out small gifts for the family: needles for the mother, safety pins for the grandmother, razor blades for the men, and colorful balloons and small tins of Nivea cream for the daughters. In turn, two of the sisters heated bear oil on the fire and gave me a hot oil scalp treatment that brought Tsetan to tears of laughter.

India

Tsetan and I traveled through boulder-strewn Ladakhi valleys above which eagles and vultures soared in the dull wintry skies. For several days we trekked along a mountain trail without seeing anyone. Then, out of nowhere, appeared a man walking alone. He was dressed in rags and his yak boots seemed about to shred apart. He uttered low moaning sounds and refrained from speaking. He might as well have been an alien who fell like a shooting star to this place that the locals call "The Land of the Broken Moon."

Tsetan and I tried to engage him, to glean where he might have come from and where he was bound. But the man remained silent and simply stood in place for long minutes, staring at us.

Here was a man without a story, or so it seemed, without a script, without a need to justify himself. He was just there, like a lump of coal. He could have been an Einstein or a wandering Buddha. He could have been a deranged outcast or a retired professor from New Delhi out doing a "sadhu thing." He could have been insane or enlightened; maybe he was both!

And I thought to myself, who would I be if it weren't for my credit card and the pile of rupee notes in my jacket; if it weren't for my social status and privilege which allows me, an elitist traveler, to wander worldwide; if I didn't have Tsetan and his two horses? Would I not be this poor man's equal — empty with nothing to lose — there under the snow clouds beside the boulders?

Tibetan Buddhists. "Buckwheat gruel and salt tea sustain us." India

Gurung family. "Fourteen days to Kathmandu." Nepal

On our last night, after weeks together, I presented Tsetan with my three-piece stainless steel cooking set — an object of particular fascination to him. Inside the pot I hid twenty-five dollars. He was overwhelmed and cried profusely. That night he tried to talk to me in English for the very first time. He labored with the words, his face contorted and his eyes pleading. I think he was trying to tell me that next year, if I came back, he would take me to a distant kingdom called Zanskar.

In the morning Tsetan was to head north along the Indus River to his refugee camp, and I, west to Leh. In parting, we hugged and squeezed one another, great bear hugs full of groans and laughter. While hugging, I tried to steal his money bag from inside his cloak, and we howled with delight.

A week later, I was overjoyed to find Tsetan at my door in Leh. He had walked twelve miles from the refugee camp to bring me a present, a handsomely woven satchel that he had made from wool he had spun during our trip. He grinned and told me to look inside the bag. I rummaged around and discovered a six-sided quartz crystal. We sat on my bed holding hands, his familiar smile and squinty eyes glowing with affection. Then, just like that, he was gone. In my mind I knew I would never see him again, but as I write this years later, I do see him often — in my heart.

Nepal

While hiking in the Himalayas with my Sherpa guide, Kipa, we spent a handful of days with an old hermit. His name was Tomba and he lived with his cat in a tiny bamboo hut in the forest. There was a sign in front of his place offering overnight accommodations, but the painted letters were worn and Tomba said that we were his first guests in over two years.

Kipa and I worked beside Tomba in his gardens, digging up weeds and adding yak dung to help stimulate the growth of his pumpkins, squash, and potatoes. We also helped rebuild the sagging roof of the hut with new bamboo poles and fresh thatching.

At night Kipa took pride in cooking for the three of us — big dishes of curried rice with dried yak meat, hot dhal with garlic sauce, and pan bread. On our last evening together we each drank a bottle of beer. The slight intoxication prompted Tomba to dance with Kipa and me around a fire, the flames licking three silly men.

When it was time for sleep, we all lay down on thin bamboo mats on the earthen floor beside the fire and a languid cat. I could hear Tomba's breathing, slow and rhythmic. The amber light from the coals pulsed on the bamboo ceiling, sometimes dying to blackness and then flickering again. Moonlight shone through a small hole in the thatch and fell across us. There was cricket song too. Except for our breathing and the cricket, all was still. It was perfect, just lying there in the silence upon the cool ground.

Nepal

While hiking across the broad Kali Gandaki riverbed, I came upon a beautiful young Tibetan woman, a nun, who was walking from Dolpo to Kathmandu to begin a three-year meditation retreat.

Sheltered from the wind, I made tea for her on my primus stove and presented her a cup with some walnuts and two oranges.

She accepted demurely, then we went our separate ways.

Gajur shepard. "The Vale of Kashmir is the summer home for our animals." India

Aymara shepard. A lifetime of watching her flock. Argentina

Nepal

Two long weeks of trekking on winding mountain trails brought us to the fringe of the high Tibetan Plateau and our first Buddhist village, Pisang. Encircled by the looming peaks of Annapurna, Lamjung, and Manaslu, the village sat in a crystalline arctic desert at close to eleven thousand feet.

My greatest pleasure in Pisang was to sit with my back up against a giant pipal tree and wait for the village orphans to show up. There must have been a dozen or more in all, ragtag boys for the most part, but a few girls too. I never learned how these children had become orphaned, nor where they slept or ate. What I did know was that I had a soft spot for them.

Sitting on a stonewall that surrounded the tree, I encouraged the ragamuffins to sit on my lap or to play favorite games with me, like "This little piggy went to market." I bet them a rupee that if they could resist laughing or smiling, the prize was theirs. I could always make them laugh.

Nepal

Kipa Sherpa rapped gently on the tent flaps. He had brought hot tea and the news that a fire had been made. I lingered in my sleeping bag with worried thoughts of the day to come. Finally dawn broke clear and cold, and the first light of the sun spilled thinly onto the massive peak of Niligiri. It was bitter cold in our ravine — five below or less — and I huddled around Kipa's small fire trying to ease the chill from my bones.

We ate breakfast hurriedly. The wind had not yet come up, and we were anxious to take advantage of the calm. Climbing up to fifteen thousand feet required all the energy I could muster. My breathing was labored and painful, my legs and back ached. I had to rest every ten or fifteen steps. Kipa was at my side the whole time, encouraging me with soft words.

By midmorning we had cleared the rock-strewn lower slope of the mountain and had emerged at the edge of a vast white kingdom of snowfields and looming peaks. Now, for some reason, the trek up the newly fallen snow seemed easier. Perhaps it was the light, or lack of oxygen, but I became delirious. At these altitudes everyday worries seemed to vanish. Instead, I was completely caught up in the moment — my boots crunching on the snow, the wind tearing at my face, the weight of the pack, my straining lungs, the enveloping breadth of blue sky, the sparkling snow.

Miss Harriet Shepard. "My sister and I own 35,000 acres of ranch land." Australia

Sadhu. "Ram, Ram, Ram." India

During my stay on the Lothlorien Organic Fruit Farm in Ahuroa, I often walked down to the home of an elderly Czechoslovakian bushman (logger) named Percy Toloph. I would help him bring his nine brindled cows in from pasture. Percy was a rugged, handsome man who always wore tall rubber boots, puffy trousers, and a rainbow-colored wool beret the women at the Farm had knitted for him. He walked with a swagger, his muscular body lumbering from side to side. Percy had a wife, though somehow I kept missing her. "Oh, the Missus is down to Warkworth doing the shopping. She'll be along soon."

When Percy came to the Farm, either to help the young folks milk cows or do some excavating with his bulldozer, money never changed hands. The Farm people "paid" Percy by cooking him dinners of roast chicken with gravy and garden vegetables, blackberry pie and fresh whipped cream for dessert. He would linger after the meal over coffee and a smoke. In the lamplight, with a child or two on his lap, Percy and the Farm folks would talk for hours. As he was leaving, someone inevitably put a loaf of freshly baked bread under his arm. "Me Missus will surely appreciate this," he would say on his way out.

For the month I stayed at the Farm, it was always "The Missus" this and "The Missus" that. Finally I asked a worker why Percy's Missus was never to be seen. "Crikey, didn't you know? There is no Missus. It's a thirty-year-old joke. He's a dyed-in-the-wool bachelor. You got took, Ethan, like hundreds before you."

Street orphans. "What do we have to look forward to, like you do?" Senegal

Maori boys at the fishing hole. New Zealand

New Zealand

I traveled to the remote East Cape of North Island. I wanted to spend time with the Maori people. In a village called Ruatahuna the school's principal allowed me to pitch my tent at the end of the ball field. On the very first day two girl students, Pae Teka and Peho, invited me to the funeral of their grandmother. I gladly accepted.

Maori funerals are held in village maraes, large wooden buildings with carved totems on the roofs depicting myths, gods, and demons. People began arriving in the afternoon, some in funky old gas-guzzling, chrome-plated barges with eight or ten people stuffed inside. Others arrived on horseback, small wiry men with thin mustaches in ill-fitting suits and, riding sidesaddle, large comely women in flowery dresses. Outside, bare-chested men as huge as sumo wrestlers cooked whole pigs and sides of beef on spits and roasted goat, chicken, turkey, and possum in great earthen pits.

Inside the marae — in the course of three days — I found the heart of Maori culture. Three hundred mattresses had been laid out on the spacious floor so that friends, family, and visitors could live together and share memories while gathered around the body and soul of the old woman.

At night, groups of women began weeping and wailing, while men and children circled them chanting ancient Maori blessings. There was much touching, young children stroking the arms and faces of their parents. How I envied them! Funerals in my culture are 45-minute cut-and-dried affairs, barren and impersonal, utterly lacking the empathy and tight tribal connectedness of the Maori.

Laba Siga game. They were perched like birds in the warm sun. Eqypt

Joanne and Opal at Lothlorien Commune. Trying to catch Leopard.
New Zealand

Australia

The Aboriginal encampments that ringed Alice Springs were desperate places, dilapidated clusters of cardboard and tin where men and women lived in squalor. Most were from nearby tribes like the Anmatjera or the Warlpiri, unable to get back to their reserves out of apathy or lack of funds.

At night the women got drunk on beer and brawled in the streets. During the day bands of hungry-looking men in rags roamed the city with looks of confusion in their wild eyes. Weary old men sat in circles, eating gristly meat and gnashing bones they had scavenged from the slaughterhouse.

When I saw how malnourished and hungry they were, I began carrying knapsacks full of food to them: cheese and sandwich meats, fruit and yogurt, cold milk for the dehydrated babies, tea and biscuits for the old men. For several weeks I made daily visits to the encampments. I joined them on their stone piles and kept vigil with them — for what, I am not sure. I would just show up and sit there, feeling lost, like them.

Native culture was dying a slow, horrifying death in Alice Springs. Nomadic life, art, dance, music, oral history – all that had meaning for the Aborigines, stretching back 50,000 years — was slipping through their fingers like sand. Most seemed resigned to the death of their world. Perhaps their acquiescence stemmed from their belief that this life is a mere shadow of real life which can only be found in the Dreamtime.

Roy Parker. "I can't read or write but I can tear down a Catepillar D3 in a day." New Zealand

Maori Man. "I have tattoo done to honor my ancestors." New Zealand

Australia

Kaapa and his people were thoroughly disoriented and marginalized by the white man's world of laws and ordinances and private ownership. For tens of thousands of years — long before the advent of cattle and mining — Alice Springs had been, for the Aborigines of the central desert, a shrine, a hallowed source of game and water, inspiration for myths and ceremonies. It was now occupied by a culture whose concepts were *totally incomprehensible* to them. Signs in storefronts read: "Proper Dress Code Enforced for Admittance" or "Pressed Pants and Collared Shirts Required." Such edicts disqualified most of the resident natives from entry or involvement in anything "white." They were now dumbfounded outcasts in their own land.

When I sat with the Aborigines on the stone piles under the eucalyptus trees, sometimes five hours at a time, they might as well have been statues for the amount they moved. There was a ghost-like quality about them, as if their bodies were still earthbound, but their souls had long since vanished. Were they dreaming? Were they beaming themselves up on a different frequency, living in another dimension? I always found myself cheering for them but was utterly mystified by them.

French Polynesia

I lived three weeks on Nuku Hiva in the Marquesas, camping in a tent under palm trees close to the turquoise waters of the sea. My nearest neighbor was an enchanting old lady named Marie Lorette who hunted for fish and octopus in a shallow lagoon nearby. Nearing 70, she was a physically strong, fiercely independent woman who had been born on the island and remained there all her life.

I seldom saw Marie Lorette with other people. She appeared to love her solitary life, daily stalking her quarry in the lagoon, her sarong pulled up to her knees, a long stick in her hand, and a fisherman's knife at her waist. She lived without electricity, cooked her fish and bread on a wood fire, and used an old white horse to make her one-hour ride over the mountains for staples.

She fished at dawn, when mists would often swirl down from the jagged peaks, blanketing her from view. As she made her way out on the reef, her figure became a mere speck. In the afternoon, wading back to the beach with her catch of octopuses strung around her waist, she would laugh, call out to me in Marquesan, and gesture that we would eat well that night.

Rua's family. The first grandchild had just arrived. Western Samoa

Dennie. "Hunting the wild pigs, eating them...It is my religion!"
The Marquessas of French Polynesia

French Polynesia

On the island of Nuku Hiva in the Marquesas Islands, I spent considerable time with the local dogs. I found them more interesting, warmer, and more communicative than the humans.

"Do dogs have Buddha Nature?" Indeed!

Kingdom of Tonga

In the village of Fakakaai on the island of Ha'ano, an old grandfather named Niu took his grandson to his gardens every morning, as if he were a school master teaching a pupil his daily lesson.

"Here is taro and here is yam. Here are the fallen seeds of hibiscus and the roots of frangipani. This plot of earth needs more compost and that plot over there needs chicken manure. Now tell me boy, what is the name of this tree and when can you expect fruit from that one?"

Even though Niu's legs and hips hurt him and he walked with a labored gait, he felt it imperative to instruct the boy about where food and medicine could be found in case the big tanker ships ran out of diesel and stopped making calls to the islands.

Sri Lanka

While in Ambepussa, I grew very fond of a diminutive eleven-year-old monk with a shaved head and sparkling eyes. He was in charge of the temple keys and was usually the one who opened and closed the door for me. The first time I saw him, I knew he was special. There was something about him that was so simple and authentic. When he walked through the gardens and bent to smell a flower, or when he stopped and patted a dog on its head, he was completely absorbed in the action. He was the closest thing I have experienced to a living Buddha. Every time I saw him, I wanted to run up and hug him and run my hand over his smooth head. When he took me to the temple and unlocked the door to let me meditate in the morning, I touched my forehead to the hem of his robe, the customary deference shown monks.

Maria Quechua, living the old Inca ways, body and soul. Bolivia

Buddhist monk. Calligraphy in the monastery. Sri Lanka

Sri Lanka

In Ambepussa I climbed a narrow wooded trail to a promontory where I sat in the sunshine eating bananas found growing along the path. When I stood up to continue on, I turned to discover a handful of boys in sarongs staring at me. They were motionless and silent, grinning broadly. I smiled back at them and wished them good morning. One boy called out to me as if he was reciting his English lesson. "Hello, Mister, I am fine. Where are you? Good-bye. Thank you." The children then laughed until self-consciousness got the best of them. Within minutes they encircled me, touching my skin and staring up at my blue eyes in amazement.

A twelve-year-old boy with a bicycle offered to drive me down to the rice paddies on his handlebars. I accepted, but wondered why I had when I found myself unpleasantly perched on the uncomfortable things. I warned him that I did not want any accidents, but he only laughed as he pushed off. We were soon speeding down the bumpy trail, careening around sharp corners, forcing old men and women, cats and dogs, chickens, and even an oxcart loaded with grain to pull aside as we whizzed by. Tears streamed down my face, turning the scenery into a chaotic blur. I screamed to the boy to put on the brakes, but he just laughed. Finally at the bottom of the hill, we coasted onto the flats. I too was laughing now, and when the bike had come to a halt, we fell over sideways onto the ground in hysterics. "Why didn't you put on your brakes and slow us down?" I asked him. He turned to me with mischievous eyes and said, "No brakes."

Vermont, USA

My closest neighbor in Washington was John Doyle. He and I lived beside each other for eighteen years. Even though he is now gone and his ashes have been scattered around his old sway-backed house, I still call out to him as I take an evening walk. "Johnny, Johnny, whatja' doin' inside? Come on out and swing in the lawn chair with me the way we used to on them hot summer days."

John was an old Swamp Yankee who spent his whole life farming hereabouts. When he was a teenager, he used to ride a big workhorse up to the high pastures to bring down the cows for evening milking.

John had a major speech impediment — he was tongue-tied — and it was always difficult to understand him. But his mind was sharp, and the joke often fell on others.

One day I had to take John to the oculist as his eyes were constantly watering. As we were driving through Barre, John belted out, "Ah don't know why ma eyes hab wader runnin' down tem all da time?"

"I know why, John. You've been having too much sex. It'll do it to you every time."

To which John retorted, with a sly grin on his whiskered face, "If dat be true, you otta be blind."

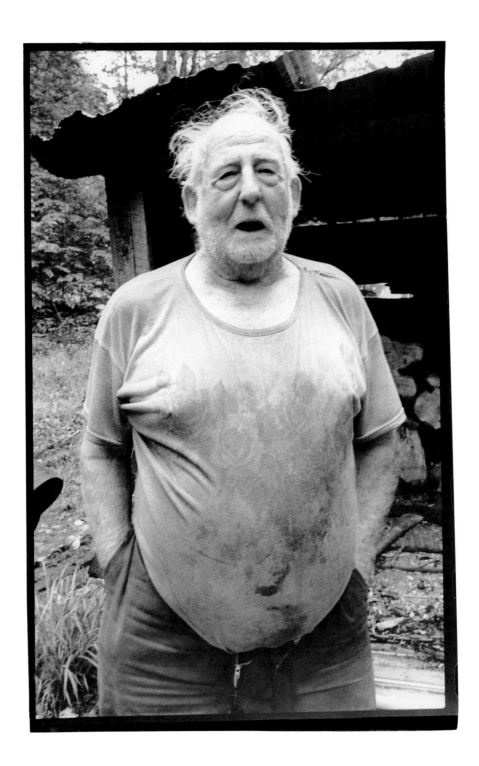

Vermont, USA

Down the hill from my house in Washington, live the Bramans, an old Vermont family that has lived and farmed in this hollow since 1802. Bill Braman, 51, is the farm's herdsman.

One day I saw Bill's father, Howard, walking down Main Street in Montpelier. I rolled down my car window and shouted a greeting to him. "Howard! Nice to see you in town."

The following day I saw Howard in the milking parlor of his farm. He was washing the equipment after morning chores. "Howard, it was great seeing you in Montpelier yesterday. First time I've ever seen you there."

Howard turned to me with warm, innocent eyes and a smile on his face, "Oh, I don't go to town if I can help it. Ya' know, I was born right here on the farm and never did leave. Everything I want is right here. This old dirt road, my family, the cows, the hills and streams, good neighbors, the turning of the seasons. Gawd, I even like 'mud season'. Guess there's no place I'd rather be than right here. Nowhere!"

Vermont, USA

From the moment I first picked up Keith Perkins and his bicycle in a blizzard on the Gulf Road, he became my teacher and special friend. With only some of his synapses firing, he was not earth-bound — freed from the self-conscious constraints common to the rest of us.

Having quit school after second grade, he now lived alone in his parent's old farm, raising potatoes, hiring out as a farm hand, collecting cans and bottles from the roadside, and cleaning public toilets. "How do you like cleaning toilets, Keith?"

"Wha?"

After repeating the question three or four times, I might finally get him to smile and reply, "It good work."

From time to time he would pedal the 26 miles from East Brookfield to Montpelier just to sip Pepsi at Charlio's honky-tonk. He would always sit alone in a corner and grin vacantly, innocently, listening to the bands and shooting Polaroids of the ceiling. Customers and staff called him "Happy."

At any time of year, Keith was apt to get on his bike and ride fourteen miles to Barre to tank up on coffee and blueberry "muppins." He would ride home in the dark, chain smoking, bundled in three layers of winter jackets, often pushing the fifty pound bike up the hills. No lights, of course. He would coast downhill, tears streaming from the cold. What was he thinking? *Was he thinking?*

"What time did you finally get home, Keith?"

"Wha?"

Vermont, USA

Jim Hayward had an accident at an early age that damaged his thinking. He struggled in school and never got past sixth grade. Like Keith Perkins, Jim was a few marbles short and for that reason the two of them connected in a special way. It slayed me when they shook hands with one another with their left hands.

One day I took Jim and Keith to the Food Coop in Montpelier for lunch. Neither of them, of course, had ever heard of tempeh or tofu. They stood in line silent and confused, like aliens just landed on a foreign planet. Finally, unable to contain himself Jim blurted out, "I ain't eatin' any of this shit." They ended up dining on slices of apple pie smothered in pickles and beets.

One evening I made reservations for the three of us at an elegant Thai restaurant. The owner eyed us suspiciously as we entered. After we were seated, the waitress recited the night's menu. To Jim and Keith everything she said was gobbledygook. Frustrated and impatient, Jim finally screamed to the owner, "Got any hot dogs?"

On the way home after the meal, Jim joined me up front, while Keith rode contentedly in back nibbling on pad tai from a doggie bag. Jim got fidgety, said he didn't get enough for dinner and was still hungry. Next thing I know he was rasping at Keith, "Hey, peckerhead, what you got back there that you ain't sharin? Pass some up here." With the moon shining in on us, and Keith repeating "Wha?" and Jim squawking like a parrot, I thought to myself, "Hell, have I died and gone to heaven?"

Vermont, USA

I met Norm Fletcher at the Montpelier farmer's market where he was selling homemade birdhouses. Chatting him up, I learned that he had once farmed in the Chelsea Hills and that he and Johnny Doyle had put up hay together back in the early 50's. They had not seen each other since. "By gawd, it'd be good to see old Johnny again after all these years," Norm ventured.

Two weeks later I arranged for Johnny, Norm, and me to have lunch in Chelsea. Over fish and chips, eggs and red flannel hash, the men spoke — loud and freewheeling — while the other diners listened enthralled. "Weren't them good old days, John? Us out under that big sky. Hard work, boy, but fun times too. Remember them jokes we told in the fields. Hell, seems like yestiddy, don't it?"

Norm begins another story as the men dive into big slices of lemon meringue pie. "John, 'member the day Bill Melvin joined us hayin'? That'd be 'bout 1953 'cause we was both using Farmall H tractors back then. Crimus, it were hot! Them two cases of Ballantine Ale that we stashed down in the crik done saved the day. Somehow we still got the job done, swingin' them bales up on the wagon. At the end of the day, you was so pickled we piled you in the bucket of the tractor to bring you home. Dumped you out like a sack of spoiled cabbages at Ginny's feet. Christ she were mad! She called you a drunken old fool and told you to spend the night with the coons and skunks." The room shook with the men's laughter. I looked at them and mused that God wasn't making these kind of Vermonters anymore.

Vermont, USA

My best friend is old Francis Foster. He is a lifeline to the past, a patchwork of old Vermont characters — logger, blacksmith, teamster, sugarer, dairyman. Francis knows how they used to roll, not plow, the winter roads, how pioneers had a trap door in the cellar to escape marauding Indians.

Francis lives alone now in Walden with his memories. His wife of 64 years died in 2008. He met and fell in love with Ginnie when he was 19, and together they raised 16 children. The old family sawmill is now derelict, the work horses long gone, but Francis, at 88, still rides about the property on an ancient Farmall H tractor. He knows every tree on his 350 acres and with his six sons still helps put up firewood for sugaring in the spring.

The day this photograph was taken Francis was showing me the old bridge that the St. Johnsbury & Lamoille County Railroad constructed across a wetland. As we walked along the ties, Francis pointed out fields where he had once gathered hay with neighboring farmers back in the 1940's.

I visit old Francis as often as I can. He is tender and fatherly to me. I'll often take a nap on his sweet-smelling bed before we eat or go down to the woodshed and examine axe handles he has made. He is not the least embarrassed by my overt show of affection. I can hug and kiss him on the cheek and tell him that I love him, and he returns the sentiment as if I were his own son.

Courtesy of Melissa Fisher

Vermont, USA

Old Harry, my adoptive father has died. I went to his funeral in Waitsfield and wept, and did so again at the auction of his things. I purchased his old # 29 Waitsfield baseball uniform and his glove. I go to his grave often to sit with him, drink a Miller High Life with him, and tell him how the Boston Red Sox are doing.

The day before he died in the hospital up to Berlin, I went to see him. He was in the intensive care unit and seemed unconscious, his breathing labored. I wept openly. It was the end of the life of my best friend. My tears spilled down my cheeks and landed smack on Harry's face, at which point he awoke with a start and chirped spryly:

"Hey, Hubbard. You don't look so good. Better get in that bed over there and spend the night with me here. No need you getting behind the wheel of your car in your broke condition. Did I ever tell you how much I like this hospital? They got these nurses who bathe me real good every night — and they don't leave no part untouched!"

Courtesy of Melissa Fisher

AFTERWORD

Now in my 70th year, my portraits have begun to stare back at me like a self-fulfilling prophecy. I seem to have become one of the eccentric old characters in my book. Call me archaic but, like them, I am hopelessly lost in the "digital age" and have no interest in its electronic marvels. I'll take a splitting maul, a wood stove, an oil lamp, a privy, and an elfin hut in a mountain pasture over the wired world any day.

Have I become "Old Harry," or "Che," or Marie Lorette? Am I too now a remnant, a relic, a curiosity? I hope so. I can't think of better company to go out with.